# Praise for *How to Take Care of Old People Without Losing Your Marbles*

"Finally, a book that tackles the subject of planning for your senior years in a concise, practical and resourceful manner. I have worked in the geripsychology field for over 20 years and this is the best resource I have found to give to families who often find themselves in need of a crash course in eldercare."

— Dr. Dahle Lattie
Geriatric Clinical Psychologist, Dallas, TX

"This book offers a great overview of aspects involved in the care of a senior. It is a rich resource for the senior themselves, their children, extended family and even neighbors or friends who may be involved in helping create a plan for the latter years of their lives. Suzanne does a great job of keeping a potentially heavy subject light-hearted and easy to read. The appendix is full of great resources for more in-depth needs. I highly recommend this book for every senior patient and their caregiver."

— Janna D. Ver Miller, MD
Geriatric Physician
at Senior Health First, Lakewood, Colorado

# How To
# Take Care of
# OLD PEOPLE
## Without
# Losing
# Your
# Marbles

# How To
# Take Care of

A
Practical
Guide to
Eldercare

# OLD PEOPLE

## *Without*

# Losing
# Your
# Marbles

*Just in time to save you (and them) –
no matter where you are in the
eldercare journey!*

## Suzanne Asaff Blankenship

How To Take Care of Old People Without Losing Your Marbles
A Practical Guide to Eldercare
by Suzanne Asaff Blankenship

Published by

Indiana Street Press Ltd.
P. O. Box 18164, Golden, CO  80402

Cover and Interior layout: Nick Zelinger, NZGraphics.com
Editing: James Hallman, WriteWorksEditing.com

ISBN: 978-0-9963739-0-6 (print)
ISBN: 978-0-9963739-1-3 (ebook)

Library of Congress Control Number: 2015916478

First Edition

Printed in the United States of America

The content of this book, including information related to health
conditions, products, and so on, is for informational purposes only,
and not meant as medical advice. You are encouraged to continue to
consult with your physicians regarding any therapies or treatments
you wish to pursue to address any elderly-related issues.

Nothing stated within this book is intended to be, and must not
be taken to be, the practice of medicine or counseling care. The
information contained within is not a substitute for, nor does it
replace, professional medical advice, diagnosis, or treatment.
Every effort has been made to provide up-to-date information, but
information and guidelines will change. It is the responsibility of the
reader to verify the most recent information for their situation.

This book is dedicated to my mom, Ruth M. Asaff. She has kept me laughing throughout with her wit, her perseverance, and her attitude towards aging. Sometimes, the laughing came afterwards – but it always came. Thanks, Mom, for giving me this opportunity to learn, grow, and share.

# Contents

Introduction . . . . . . . . . . . . . . . . . . . . . . . . . . . . . 1

**1  Calling Their Bluff**
*Evaluating their needs* . . . . . . . . . . . . . . . . . 7

**2  Prepare, Prepare, Prepare**
*The key to getting started* . . . . . . . . . . . . . 15

**3  Putting Your Nose in Their Business**
*Power of Attorney/legal documents* . . . . . 21

**4  Money Doesn't Grow on Trees**
*Financial evaluation* . . . . . . . . . . . . . . . . . . . 29

**5  Saving Grace (or Mom, Whichever Comes First)**
*Long-Term Care insurance* . . . . . . . . . . . . . 41

**6  Finding a Place to Park Them**
*Housing options* . . . . . . . . . . . . . . . . . . . . . . . 55

**7  Medicare Made Simple (Yeah, Right!)**
*Important Medicare basics* . . . . . . . . . . . . . 67

## 8 This is Your Parent on Drugs...
*Prescription drug management
and insurance*. . . . . . . . . . . . . . . . . . . . . . . .  79

## 9 The Missing Link
*Medical coordination and advocacy*. . . . .  85

## 10 Hiring a Nanny
*Home health care options*. . . . . . . . . . . . . .  89

## 11 Getting Ready to Host The Antiques Roadshow™
*Sorting and dealing with "treasures"*. . . .  95

## 12 The "No Sale" Look and the "Huh?" Expression
*Helping them help you and themselves*. . .  101

## 13 Sibling Rivalry
*How to share the care* . . . . . . . . . . . . . . . .  107

## 14 The Topic No One Wants to Discuss – Hospice
*Important facts and options* . . . . . . . . . .  111

## 15 The Exit Ramp
*Death, cremation/donation/
burial, services.* . . . . . . . . . . . . . . . . . . . . . . 123

## 16 Dealing with the Remains
*What to do with possessions after
they pass* . . . . . . . . . . . . . . . . . . . . . . . . . . . 129

## 17 The Fat Lady is Just Getting Warmed Up!
*Task list for wrapping up business
after death* . . . . . . . . . . . . . . . . . . . . . . . . . 135

## 18 The Final Chapter
*The last hoorah before launching
the process* . . . . . . . . . . . . . . . . . . . . . . . . . 143

Resources for Eldercare Navigation. . . . . . . 145

Acknowledgments. . . . . . . . . . . . . . . . . . . . . . 159

About the Author. . . . . . . . . . . . . . . . . . . . . . 161

How to Connect with Suzanne. . . . . . . . . . . 163

# Introduction

It came upon me both suddenly and at a snail's pace. My mother has had good health for most of her life and has achieved the age of 97 without much of a long, slow decline. In that, we were fortunate. However, as I was born when she was 45, and didn't start my own family until I was 42, I am the perfect example of the so-called Sandwich Generation.

My mother and I live in different states. As a widow from the age of 49 and of the "older generation," my mother has needed care and guidance for years on certain things (business, electronics, finances, etc.). I expected that and have been helping her with those things for years. What took me by surprise were her declining capabilities in the things she had always done well (cooking, cleaning, painting, getting dressed up, etc.).

After I flew down for her emergency pacemaker surgery, I saw this decline first-hand, happening right in front of me in full bloom. At the time, I thought most of her challenges had to do with the surgery and hospital stay. After a visit at Thanksgiving, I saw that she was forgetting to pay bills, not preparing or eating meals, and was getting her

1

medications confused. This vexed my mom as much as it did me.

It was then that I began to assume the "full caretaker" role and to manage these responsibilities from far away. Much of the time, it felt like I was the remote operator of the submarine trying to turn off the valves of the BP oil spill.

After a few years of this project with my own mom, we moved my in-laws from another state to a new place within a mile of our house. Immediately, my father-in-law was diagnosed with cancer and needed radiation therapy. My mother-in-law looked to my husband (and to me) to coordinate the medical procedures, doctor visits, and treatment – all of it. This was my first experience with caretaking in such close proximity. I had turned face-first into a fire hydrant stream of need. And my 6 year old had not stopped needing me either!

My mom used to point to older folks who were struggling and say to me "if I ever get to that point, just shoot me!" Well, that's not an option! Over the years, the caretaking can get just about that frustrating for all involved. I've managed to laugh at her comment instead of crying (most times anyway). This book is intended to help you do the same.

While humor helps tame the moment, organization and preparation are the keys to successful navigation of eldercare issues. With over 20 years of business experience, I put my organization and project management to work on each of my eldercare issues. This is not your typical eldercare approach; but it is one that works. When you approach eldercare as a project to be organized and managed, it also helps mitigate the emotional strain and frustration.

It is from this perspective and this set of learning experiences that I offer you ideas and thought-provoking suggestions for navigating eldercare. And, most of all, some support for the job that will feel like it could take you over the edge of sanity.

It is my intent that this book is, above all, practical. You don't need more useless advice (you've got all those cable TV shows for that). You need down-and-dirty information straight from the trenches; you need driving directions for eldercare. Well, lucky you, here it is!

For those of you who have not yet begun the roller coaster ride of eldercare, you can use this book to plan, to get yourself prepared, and to help guide your parents to the best launching point for their golden years.

For those of you who have joined us in the middle of the Class IV whitewater rapids of caretaking (that's Westerner speak for craziness), go to the chapter that deals with your current issues and questions. Go back and forth in the book as your needs dictate. It can be a guidebook and a map for the part of the journey that you are living now.

Congratulations on picking up this book, on taking an interest in your parents' well-being and in your own well-being, for this impacts you as much as it impacts your parents. Be open and honest with yourself on how this feels. It is often a dichotomy of love and frustration.

When in doubt, laugh. Give up on perfection in this endeavor and shoot for balance. It is tough. These are people you care about. The tables are turned – they need you now. Walk into it with your eyes open, your mind prepared, and your running shoes on – it is a marathon, not a sprint. You will finish and you will be glad you paced yourself. There won't be a medal, but you will have a strong sense of accomplishment and a few marbles left too.

SAB
The Eldercare Navigator

# It might be helpful to know...

## *What This Book Is Not* –

- Not a substitute for professional advice on legal, financial, medical, governmental, or psychological issues
- Not a comprehensive text on everything that you will encounter in eldercare
- Not a resource for any topics on dementia
- Not a summary of Medicare, Medicaid, or Social Security
- Not a substitute for anything official on government programs
- Not meant to provide customized answers to unique situations.

## *What This Book Is* –

- A guide to help navigate the biggest issues in eldercare
- A resource for ideas and suggestions on common situations that occur in the lives of the elderly
- A way to organize your thoughts and prepare for frequent elder topics
- A tool to refer to when confronted with a new eldercare dilemma

- A planning reference for folks who want to be prepared for helping their parents or other elders in the coming years
- A great way to find humor in the face of a very tough subject.

Now, as your eldercare navigator, I'm going to help you put some marbles back into your bag and some sanity back into your life!  Start navigation...

"Sure, I always use online banking."

# Chapter 1

# Calling Their Bluff

**O**kay – so our parents are the folks who always had the answer. Right? They gave their opinions as though they were speaking the Gospel truth (true or not). Then, they raised you to spit out the answers for your kids the same way.

Guess what? They still think they have the answers. And now that they're getting older, your job is to see which ones they really do have and on which ones they are bluffing. Because, believe me, when your parents get older, *they are bluffing* about some things! Wouldn't you? I mean, if things started falling off the hanger, so to speak, like they do when you start to hit those "golden years," you'd bluff too.

What might they be bluffing about?

## Finances

- They have plenty of money to last through their lifetime.
- They remember to pay their bills and renew their licenses.

- They still diligently comparison shop – on things like insurance, services, and when confronted by unsolicited sales pitches.
- They routinely shred confidential information.
- They can effectively identify which charities are worthwhile and how much to give them.
- They keep their wills (including living wills and powers of attorney) up-to-date and know where they are.

# Self-Care

- They know how to thoroughly wash their hands.
- They eat three meals per day.
- They can take their meds in order and at the right time.
- They renew prescriptions before they run out.
- They clean their kitchens, bathrooms, and the floors.
- They can see the dust and it bothers them.
- They bathe regularly.
- They change their toothbrushes.
- They can see stains on their clothes and it bothers them.
- They can clip their toenails.

## Medical

- They can go to the doctor and still remember to follow the instructions when they get home.
- They can remember why they made the appointment in the first place (when they called two months ago).
- They give accurate and succinct (well...) descriptions of symptoms and concerns to their doctor.
- They understand the instructions given to them by the doctor (when they can remember them).
- They can distinguish between the need for a doctor and the need for a Band-Aid® or Tylenol®.
- They don't ask the cardiologist about things that the urologist should examine (My mom's cardio doc told her that was below his pay grade!).

## Orientation

- They can go to new places and follow directions to get to them.
- They can go to favorite places and return home safely.

- They can make left turns from the left lane.
- They can still merge into traffic without causing an accident.
- They remember where their car is parked at the mall.
- They can go the speed limit (all the way up to the speed limit, I mean).
- They know who to call for help when they can't do one of the above.

## Safety and Security

- They lock their doors at home. They lock their car doors. (Unless they live in rural Iowa.)
- They don't let strange salespeople come in and visit in the living room.
- They keep their valuables hidden and/or locked in a safe.
- They sleep with their windows open only if they are above the first floor or they have window stops to prevent entry.
- They don't forget their purse very often or leave the credit card at the store.
- They keep their keys in one place so they can find them.

# Rubble

- There is no bluffing on this. They have tons of stuff, think of it all as valuable beyond computation, and will collect more of it.
- They said they have cleaned it all out (hint: not a chance this is true!).

Your turn to bluff here – go visit with deep pockets and large totes like you are going to the beach or the ballgame. But instead, shoplift every time you visit.

You think I'm kidding...well, I'm not! Take a very close look at your folks the next time you're over there. If you don't notice any bluffing, I've got some oceanfront real estate for you in Arizona.

It is your job to figure out how much each bluff is worth, and when you want to call your parents out on them. This is the tightrope you must walk in eldercare.

You know your parents and how they have always been. If they were neatniks, a flag will go up if their lives are now cluttered. It is the deviations from "normal" that you want to pay the most attention to in your evaluation.

You may do a check and find that they are not bluffing...yet. Well, then use that as a baseline and check again in one to two years.

Once you have identified where they are fine and where (or if) they need help, you can begin to make a plan to prop up their efforts with backup from you.

It's hard to get your brain around the concept of them bluffing, of them needing something really significant besides the cards, visits, and phone calls – but at some point, they will need more. It's well worth your while to stay current on this.

------------------------------------

*Old people are good at bluffing. The bluffs cover areas where they are becoming less capable. Stay one step ahead of them on this and you'll know where they will need assistance next.*

------------------------------------

# Chapter 2
# Prepare, Prepare, Prepare

**Y**ou might look at your parents' needs and think, "Not my problem." Oh sure. Yes, they are; their issues are your issues! And, the more you ignore them, the bigger they get! Just like your pants' size – if you ignore your need to be active, your problem gets bigger. The stuff that's getting harder for your folks is no different!

*You will want to prepare:*

- Their finances, for the upcoming costs of care as they get older.
- Their housing, accommodating for current needs and preparing for the future as well.
- Their paperwork, for allowing your participation in their life decisions with a power of attorney, and for making sure their wills and living wills are current.
- Their minds for what is ahead, for your increased level of participation in their life decisions, and for your help in developing a plan for their golden years.

- Yourself, for seeing your parents' abilities and needs change in ways that are not expected, not pleasant, and, yet, to make those times special for you all.

Like any project you tackle, you need to be organized in order to be successful. Follow these steps:

1) Evaluate
2) Assess
3) Develop A Plan
4) Implement (sometimes Repeat)

# Evaluate

Based on the list in the last chapter, evaluate where your parents need help now, where they might need help next, and where they are functioning just fine.

Throughout the book, we will discuss specific issues of finances, housing, care services, medical issues, dying/death, and all those "other" items not in the big categories. Think of each chapter as you would a science project: what do you know, what do you need to know, what do you not know that you might need to know, and what is irrelevant?

## Assess

Once you get the information on their health, housing, finances, and care needs, you can assess how you will move forward together: by integrating what they need, what they want, and what assistance you (and, perhaps, your siblings) can provide.

## Develop A Plan

This book will give you lots of help evaluating their circumstances, along with methods to access the information you obtain, but it will be up to you (with your parents' help) to develop a personalized plan for their future. Each situation will be different (in fact, it may even be different for each parent) and will require thoughtful questions to be asked, hard topics to be discussed, and sometimes an exhaustive search for resources. Be undaunted. Approach it as if you were a detective on a difficult but important investigation (you kind of are!).

Any plan for the future will likely need to be amended as life events move around the various pieces of your plan. Be flexible! Understand that most of the events in the latter years of life are surprises and come at unexpected times.

If you have a plan, though, you have something to guide you, to inform you, and to help you as you and your parents navigate these uncharted and very emotionally-mined waters.

# Implement

Act. Move. Decide.

You cannot make a difference for your parents' future if you just look at the plan as a nice addition to your computer files or your bookshelf.

You will be so glad that you did the heavy lifting now, rather than having waited for life's surprises or for life-altering events to force you into action.

Don't be surprised if sometimes you need to reevaluate or repeat a step. (Smile, this keeps it interesting!)

Now, get your ammo, get your camouflage outfit on, and get ready to hunt – for information, for answers, for resources, for wisdom, and for the key to helping your parents while keeping your own life moving forward and your marbles in the bag.

------------------------------------

*Prepare for the future needs of your parents now. Urgent decisions and old people are not the best bedfellows.*

------------------------------------

On the "hunt" for information.

# Chapter 3

# Putting Your Nose in Their Business

Wherever your folks are on the independence scale, it is never too early to get your name as an authorized representative regarding their affairs. After all, before you can hunt for answers, you will need a permission slip. A power of attorney and/or authority to represent them is that permission slip in the eyes of the law.

Power of attorney (POA) documents are essential. This is just like having an extra key outside the house for when you lock yourself out. It helps to have it in advance of needing it!

There are two types that you should have: a "Durable Power of Attorney for Financial Management" and a "Medical Power of Attorney."

## Durable Power of Attorney for Financial Management

A durable power of attorney for financial management allows you to make decisions on behalf of your parent or parents regarding real estate, transactions and maintenance of personal property, banking affairs, business and insurance, estate/trust issues, government benefits, and retirement benefits. It also allows you to enter into claims or litigation on their behalf. You can engage in family care, tax matters, gifts, and charity issues as well as employ persons on their behalf. Unless you arrange for a medical power of attorney as well, the durable power of attorney for financial management does not allow you to make medical decisions for them.

You can hold the durable power of attorney individually or jointly with your siblings (or other guardian individuals like aunts/uncles/cousins).

A lawyer can create this document for you, or you can obtain a form from various Internet sites. Signing this document generally requires two witnesses that are not related, and it may need to be notarized. Check the requirements in your state and/or locality.

You will need to keep a copy of this document with you if you plan to conduct business on their behalf.

## Medical Power of Attorney

A medical power of attorney allows you to perform as the elder person's health care agent.

You can speak with doctors and care providers; you can see medical records and make decisions about care and treatment. (You might be tempted to order an extra shot for them from time to time...)

You can also pay their bills and talk to those lovely ladies in the billing department at doctors' offices (when they try to charge full price for things that Medicare and/or supplemental insurance covers, for example). An aside – always know the first names of those lovely ladies in the billing department and the ladies at the front desk too. You may need them in your corner at some point.

The same legal framework applies to a medical power of attorney – two witnesses who are unrelated, usually notarized. Check with your state.

## Copies – Who needs them?

*Financial Management Power of Attorney (FPOA):*

- Family Attorney
- Banks/Investment Brokers/Mutual Funds
- Real Estate Agents/Title Companies
- Pensions/Retirement Benefits Administrators
- Insurance Agencies/Brokers/Companies
- Tax Professionals/CPAs/Tax Attorneys
- Charities to which they have committed funds/gifts

- Housing/Landlord/Residence Owners
- State and local records departments

*Medical Power of Attorney (MPOA):*
- Doctors/Medical Clinics/Hospitals
- Home Health Care Agencies
- Insurance Companies
- Pharmacies/Prescription Insurance Companies
- Housing/Retirement Residences
- Dentists/Audiologists/Eye Care Professionals
- Senior Centers

Some of these people/organizations may have their own forms that they want you to complete in addition to keeping a copy of your POA form.

## Government and POAs

Most government agencies do not recognize power of attorney forms. Instead, they have their own forms and processes for allowing access to your parents' files and transactions. Specific website information is listed in the Resources section in the back of this book.

Social Security has a special form called Form SSA 1696 that allows someone to represent you on a variety of issues. Go to the Social Security website and search for the form. The instructions for completing and submitting this form, along with explanations about what topics can be handled by an authorized representative, are clear enough and shouldn't cause you too much trouble.

Medicare has a form called an "Authorization to Disclose Personal Health Information" (CMS-10106) that allows Medicare to discuss medical information with someone other than the insured. You can find this form at the Medicare website along with instructions on how to complete and submit it.

The Veterans Administration (VA) uses VA Form 21-0845 – called an "Authorization to Disclose Personal Information to a Third Party." You can locate this form at the VA website and search by form number. This will need to be mailed, faxed, or delivered to the VA office.

In case you want the VA to release your parent's medical information to you or to a medical provider, you will want to use VA Form 10-5345, a "Request For and Authorization to Release Medical Records of Health Information." This one allows the VA to release medical records and health information to an authorized person or organization. This form can also be found at the VA website. Search for the form by number.

Other government agencies may recognize the forms from Social Security, Medicare, and/or the VA; however, they may elect to use their own form. The term to ask about is the "Assignment of Personal Representative." Smaller agencies like the Bureau of Indian Affairs or the Railroad Retirement Board may accept the forms from the larger agencies, but it is best to ask about this with each agency that affects your parents.

## Usage

No matter how many forms you have, your parents still have the authority to make decisions on their own behalf. Your POA (power of attorney) can be changed or revoked at any time. A POA is always granted at their discretion, and is to be used as needed by them or by you, especially if they need decisions to be made and are temporarily (or permanently) unable to make them.

Some parents are more than willing to extend power of attorney and some are more hesitant. There are times when it might be helpful (like if they go to the hospital and you need to make a decision for them while they are under anesthesia), or instances where they might want you to sell something for them (like property, their car, or some furniture). Discuss these potential situations and how having a POA will help you both.

## Advance Directive

At some point, you will want to discuss an advance directive with them. This form specifies the circumstances under which your parent wants intervention to prevent death and when they do not, as well as telling caregivers what kind of end-of-life care they want. Sometimes this is called a "Do Not Resuscitate Order" or DNR. For example, an advance directive would specify in what instances a feeding tube would be allowed or when it wouldn't. The same goes for a ventilator and other lifesaving measures. It is imperative that your parent keep a copy of this document with them at all times. If they are in an ambulance on their way to the hospice center and have no document, the ambulance paramedics would likely be required to resuscitate them in the event of a life-threatening situation, whether or not that was your parent's preference. Every state has its own procedures around this type of form. Check with your parent's healthcare provider, residence facility, or attorney for more information.

Putting your nose in their business can be stinky at times but it helps to be able to sniff out where they need help and where they are still capable of dealing with their own "creations." Just remember the reasons and excuses you invented to get a key to your parent's car when you turned 16 – use that same resourcefulness now to gain access to their affairs in case it's needed.

----------------------------------

*It is never too early to get both durable financial and medical powers of attorney. They do not have to be used until they are needed.*

----------------------------------

# Chapter 4
# Money Doesn't Grow on Trees

Even if it did, your parents are in the autumn of their lives and the leaves are falling off at a record pace! Everyone likes to think that this is the part that will take care of itself – the money to live comfortably during his or her golden years will be abundant and flow smoothly. Not! Well, not if you don't evaluate, assess, and develop a financial plan.

Unlike health issues or the death of a spouse, money issues should not be surprises and should not happen suddenly. Your best defense for your parents to survive and thrive financially is for you to have a clear understanding of their current and future income stream (hope they have big, thick branches on their money tree) as well as having a good grasp of their current and potential expenses. That way, you can plan to water, fertilize, and prune as needed.

## Evaluate

Remember my list from the "Prepare" chapter? Well, it's critical here. You need to sit down with your parents right now and get a complete picture of their financial situation. You may need that power of attorney to get some of this info.

Start with this list and add based on your parents' individual situations.

- Identify bank accounts (savings, checking, money market, CDs) and get the balances. Do they have direct deposits coming in monthly or quarterly? Do they use electronic bill pay? Find out what gets paid.

- Get balances and statements for investments of all kinds (stocks, bonds, mutual funds, annuities, IRAs, retirement funds). What do they own, how liquid are the investments, and what degree of risk do they carry? What interest income and dividend income do they make? Get the name and contact info of their investment advisor.

- Obtain pension information. What is the status of their pension now; how can it change in the future? What is the risk to the pension if their old employer gets into trouble? Do surviving spouses get the full pension or is it reduced upon the death of the earning spouse?

- What is the amount of Social Security benefit that each parent receives each month? Get a copy of the annual benefit statement that Social Security sent them for last year.

- Do they receive Veterans Administration benefits? If so, how much monthly? Are there requirements to file forms annually or periodically? Are they filing those forms? Get copies.

- Do they have income from inheritance or trusts? Get amounts.

- What medical insurance do they have? Is it through a former employer, Medicare, and/or supplemental insurance company? Get a copy of their insurance cards and Medicare cards for your files. What is their monthly premium if they have supplemental insurance (other than Medicare)? Is there a copay or a deductible to be met for care? Get the exact amounts – they may be different for primary care, specialists, hospitals, ERs, and urgent care clinics. If they have Medicare, what plan are they on? Do they have a Medicare Advantage plan instead? It would be helpful to have a list of medical expenses for the last two years. This helps in case you need to file for VA benefits or substantiate tax deductions.

- What prescription drug insurance do they have? Do they have it together with their medical insurance or is it part of a separate plan? What is their monthly premium and how is it paid? What drugs do they take and what is their out-of-pocket monthly cost? Do they order from a local pharmacy? Mail order? Both? Get a list.

- What insurance coverage do they have for dental/vision/hearing? Medicare does not cover most of these items. Coverage usually comes with a supplement and/or previous employment coverage. This stuff gets expensive! Ask your parents what they have spent over the last two to three years on these items. Hearing aids can run $7000, dental implants several thousand, even glasses can run into the hundreds too.

- What real estate do they own? Get copies of deeds. What is this property worth? How easily can it be sold if funds are needed? Do they have a reverse mortgage that they've taken out to get liquid funds from home equity?

- What personal property do they own of significant value? Cars, recreational vehicles, hobby collections, antiques, and jewelry are all examples of items of value that you will want to include and quantify in your picture of their finances.

- What are their monthly expenses for housing, food, medicine, services, insurance, cars, recreation, and other items? Make a list of monthly and periodic expenses.

- Do they have life insurance? What amount are they carrying? Is there cash value associated with their plan? If it is a term policy, when does the term expire? Get a copy of the policy.

- Do they have death and disability insurance? Understand the policy if they do.

- Do they have long-term care insurance? What requirements are there to qualify for benefits? What do they pay for and for how long? What reporting requirements are there for the patient and/or their family?

Is the policy shared or individual? Is nursing care paid at a different level than assisted living? Is home care covered at 100%, a reduced percentage, or at any level at all? Is there a waiting period before benefits are paid – i.e., do you have to pay for your care for a period of time before the long-term benefits start?

- Do they have burial insurance? What does it cover and does it limit their choices? Get a copy of the policy. Have they done any pre-planning for a funeral or memorial service? Have they paid any funds out? Do they own a cemetery plot? Get a copy of all the receipts and paperwork. Do they plan to donate their body to a scientific institution? Get the documents and instructions. If they plan on cremation or body donation, don't forget to cancel the burial insurance that they bought from the door-to-door salesperson.

- Did they file a tax return last year? Get a copy, review it, and make sure they completed it accurately. Many older folks pay too much in taxes because they don't seek advice of a tax professional or advisor (AARP and other organizations offer free advice and free/reduced fee tax preparation).

- Where are their important documents located? Make sure you have the code to the safe or the key to the safe deposit box (and know where it is!).

## Assess

Make a spreadsheet of income and expenses. Do they have enough income to cover current expenses or are they borrowing from savings every month?

How can you help them be more efficient with their expenses, extending the life of their retirement funds?

You may want to help them evaluate the risks of their investments. If they are not focused on income and have too much risk, you will want to speak to their investment advisor about matching their investment strategy to their current needs. Oftentimes, it has been years since they really went through their investments with a fine-toothed comb and looked at risk level compared to age and need for income. They may need to evaluate better vehicles for providing interest income (such as CDs, bonds, or money market funds).

Evaluating insurance coverage is a very worthwhile endeavor too. Needs change and insurance companies increase rates. Make a point to look at their home/auto/renters insurance deductibles, coverage amounts, and replacement cost coverage for an appropriate fit to current circumstances (Here's a tip: if they're still driving, you may want to increase their collision and liability coverage... a lot). Are they paying their premiums annually or monthly? There are often huge savings for paying annually or in a lump sum.

At the end of every year, people have an opportunity to review their current Medicare and prescription drug coverage, as well as their supplemental medical insurance. Compare your elders' medical expenses to their current plans and make sure that coverage matches needs. If they go to the doctor infrequently, a plan with a higher copay for each visit may cost less than a full coverage plan with no copay. The ability to purchase medications from a mail-order pharmacy may reduce prescription drug costs significantly. The Medicare website offers some helpful comparison coverage and cost charts by zip code. AARP's website offers some helpful comparisons on supplemental Medicare coverage as well.

Housing and assistance are areas of enormous cost for the elderly. Evaluate the benefits of renting versus owning, look at the costs of at-home care versus a retirement residence with assistance, and check into community services to replace an auto and associated expenses. These are all examples of how you can make sure your parents' funds are spent as efficiently as possible.

## Develop a Plan

Put together a plan for how you will work with your parents on finances. Will you review their situation once a year? Will you start helping them with major decisions? Will you look over their shoulder while they pay bills, or will you need to take over the entire process?

Generate a "what if" scenario or two. Estimate what would happen to income and expenses if one spouse died or if one spouse needed more extensive care (home aides, assisted living, more doctor visits, etc.).

Estimate what might happen if some major income source were to be reduced or go away. What adjustments could be made, what property or investments could be sold, what expenses could be reduced?

These "what-if" scenarios allow you to brainstorm with your parents without the corresponding stress of a traumatic event or situation that can cloud everyone's judgment. They can tell you what they have planned or what they would prefer to do in case of a major life change.

Getting an understanding of where they are financially is so important because it impacts their quality of life going forward... and yours too.

## Implement

Decide on what happens next. When will you begin the next steps?

Let them know what to expect from you and when to expect it.

Write down what they need to do and assign timing together.

If you have a plan, set expectations and meet them. When you do, your parents will likely have much less trepidation about your entrance into their private affairs than they would have otherwise.

Don't hesitate to reiterate what your goals are together and what they can expect from you. They may have trouble remembering what they committed to doing and/or forget to leave room for you in the process.

## What's the Point?

This exercise will be different for every family. Some may have little or no income or assets except what is provided by the government. Some may have extensive assets that they want to protect for future generations. In either case, you will want to have a complete understanding of your parents' financial situation, both now and in the future.

Preserving and protecting their money is the first step to really taking care of your parents. Without resources, the going can get really tough in old age. Lack of financial planning will take the "gold" out of their golden years for sure.

You may want to run from this; it's not my favorite fun Saturday afternoon family activity. Wading through a swamp of money matters is daunting for anyone, especially when you do it with your parents, but you have to do it! Just put on your hip-waders and grab a big fly swatter.

------------------------------------

*Build a complete picture of your elders' financial situation (assets, liabilities, commitments). Know where their important documents are stored. Don't wait until you need this information or need a document.*

------------------------------------

Martha thought Medicare would pay for
her assisted living.

Grace bought long-term care insurance.

## Chapter 5

# Saving Grace (or Mom, Whichever Comes First)

Beyond all the financial investigation that you did after reading the last chapter, beyond all your calculations, estimations, and "what-ifs," there is one saving grace that can mean the difference between comfort and anxiety, between peace and constant frustration. That grace is called long-term care (LTC) insurance.

LTC insurance has made the difference between my mom living under a bridge and living in a lovely assisted living residence with great care and services. Really...it makes that big of a difference!

It's not my job to give you financial advice – but, you do have to hear me out on this: You must look into long-term care insurance and, when you do, think not of today, tomorrow, or next year; think 10, 20, 25 years down the road. What if your parents are still living in 2030 and they have needed extensive care for years? How will they (or you) pay for it? Will there be enough resources?

There is a myth that Medicare or medical insurance pays for long-term care, the type that is expensive and extensive (think nursing home – where rates can be $200-250 or more per day). Well, that's not happening! Medicare *does not pay for long-term care*. I'd say that the idea they do is the biggest myth in eldercare today. You'll find the fountain of youth sooner than you'll get LTC paid for by Medicare or medical insurance.

If your parents want to know who *will* pay for their nursing care or assisted living care, have them pick up a mirror. They may want to join you for a collective scream.

Now, let's welcome Long-Term Grace, a lovely addition to the team.

Long-term care insurance preserves the assets your parents have, supplements resources when they don't have enough, and takes care of them when they are the most vulnerable.

Because seniors are living longer, needing more care during their longer lifetimes, and finding that care to be incredibly expensive, long-term care insurance is changing every year. Get it now! It's not likely to get any cheaper down the road.

LTC insurance generally pays benefits when your parents can no longer independently perform two or more "Activities of Daily Living" (ADLs).

ADLs are:

- Bathing (as in washing oneself, getting into/out of the bath/shower)
- Feeding (as in bringing the food to the mouth with a fork or getting formula into a feeding tube)
- Dressing (putting on and taking off clothes, including fasteners)
- Toileting (getting to and from the toilet, getting on/off the toilet, performing hygiene related to toilet)
- Continence (ability to maintain bowel and urine control and/or perform hygiene related to bowel/urine control)
- Transferring (getting into/out of a chair, bed or wheelchair)

LTC insurance also pays benefits when your parent has a cognitive impairment that requires them to be under constant supervision or when they need substantial assistance to prevent them from being a threat to their own safety or to others. Examples include cases of severe dementia or Alzheimer's disease.

## Evaluate

What type of LTC insurance do your parents need? Here are some things to consider:

- Do your parents want to live at home as long as possible?
- What is the family history of longevity? Does your family tend to live into their 90s, or do most pass away before 80?
- Would a retirement residence fit their needs better?
- Are family members willing to do much of the caretaking?
- Is their home suited for elder living? Can it be retrofitted easily and with minimal investment for elder living?
- Are they stubborn and independent about caregivers? Will they be comfortable with caregivers coming into their home?

Spend some time thinking about these questions. They will help you determine what the LTC insurance needs to cover, for how long, and in what circumstances.

## Assess

Coverage plans are designed around the time period that care will be provided, the amount of care your parents need, and the conditions under which it will be provided. Options vary by state.

LTC coverage periods range from two years to lifetime coverage (but that option is almost non-existent now). You purchase a plan that matches the length of time that you think your parents will need to be cared for before their deaths. Like any insurance, any guess you make is a gamble. The average length of stay at a nursing facility is 2-3 years, but in reality, care of all types/levels can last many years.

Amounts of coverage vary according to what you think you will need and what you can afford to pay in premiums. In your parents' city, the average daily rate of full nursing care might be as much as $250 per day right now. That's $7500 per month. Such figures vary widely by geography – some places cost substantially more and some substantially less. You'll find that costs also depend on the need for services and care. Assisted living costs less than full nursing care. In-home care can be cheaper if your parents need only a few hours of attention a day, but when they need more than about eight hours of care per day, you may find a residence facility to be more cost effective. In your LTC plan, you can purchase monthly care amounts equal to the difference between what your parents' budget allows and the actual cost of care that they'll need. For example, if their income can support $2500 per month and you estimate that it will cost $7500 per month to care for them, you can purchase $5000 per month in LTC insurance. If you can't afford the whole amount, buy as much as you can afford.

Where the care is given and under what circumstances also are factors to consider when looking at LTC insurance. Your folks can receive care in one of three main settings – nursing care facilities, assisted living facilities, and in-home/in-community care. Some policies cover assisted living and home care at a reduced percentage of benefit (typically through group policies). My recommendation is that you get all three options paid at full benefit. That way, your parents can get care in whatever setting will work best for them, without regard to the cost factor – remember, you may not know for sure what they will need when you select a policy.

The "elimination period" is the time that your parents have to pay for their own care out of pocket before the insurance begins to pay. Some policies offer a 30-day elimination period; some go out for 90 days. You will have to estimate your parents' financial situation to determine what works best for them. The elimination period can be calculated in "service days" (days that only count if your parent is receiving a service on a given day) or "calendar days" (services start on the day that the policy holder first receives service, and continue until the calendar reaches 30, 60 or 90 days hence). Plans that have shorter elimination periods usually cost more than ones with longer elimination periods. My preference is for a plan with calendar days because it is doesn't usually require services to be hired every day of the period, thus making it less expensive to get through the period than with service days.

If you get a "home care elimination period waiver," the care that your parent gets at home does not have to satisfy the elimination period (they can get a benefit on day one of need), but the days of service at home can sometimes count toward your facility elimination period. In other words, your parent could receive assistance from a home health care aide for a few hours a day, with the benefit payments starting the first time this aide comes. Then, after your facility elimination period has been satisfied for the requisite period (say 90 days), your parent could move to a facility and you would not have to pay the entire amount out of pocket. Get this waiver!

Keep in mind that all of this will happen when your parent needs care, and you have to prove to the LTC insurance company that your parent has met the criteria to begin receiving the benefits on the policy. This is not easy and can require much work to prove, depending on the insurance company in question. Their job is to keep your parent paying the premium (and not receiving benefits), while your job is to try to get the benefits when your parent needs them. You need to be determined in order to win that tug of war!

With LTC insurance, you will still need to have the financial resources set aside to care for your parents for at least 90 days – either because of the elimination period or because it can take that long to convince the insurance company that your parent qualifies for the benefit. Make sure you plan for this in their budget.

Another selection you will have to make is between a "single policy" and a "shared policy" (if there are two people involved). Shared policies allow one spouse to "borrow" funds from the pool when he/she runs out of funds from their own policy. This is helpful if your dad turns out to need a shorter period of care than your mom, for example. They could share six years – he would get two, and she would get the remaining four.

One element to make sure you have in the policy, if it is a shared policy, is a "spousal waiver of premium benefit." This option allows the spouse that is not receiving a benefit to get a waiver of premium once the other spouse begins to receive benefits. If one spouse needs care and qualifies for benefits, you want the entire premium to be waived for both if possible.

The "bed reservation benefit" allows your parent to keep their apartment/room at a facility while he/she is in the hospital, in a rehabilitation facility, or in hospice care. This is important if you don't want them to have to move out of their space while they are receiving care elsewhere temporarily.

The "hospice care benefit" allows your loved one to be cared for at an inpatient hospice facility and to be covered while there. It also covers in-home hospice care. Medicare hospice benefits only cover the medical services part of hospice, not room and board. You want this benefit!

The "respite care benefit" pays for someone else to care for your parent while the loved one who usually cares for him or her takes a few days off. This is a nice benefit if your parent's primary caretaker is a non-paid family member (like you or the other parent).

The *most important* thing to make sure you have included in the policy is "inflation protection." Costs for eldercare are going up every day, sometimes by staggering amounts. Costs that you predict your parent will need to pay today for care could be very different in 5, 10, or 15 years when they actually need care. You can choose between a 3% or a 5% inflation factor – but make sure your policy allows for compounded interest.

Benefits can be paid monthly or daily. Since most plans require that you submit actual expenses for reimbursement, I would recommend selecting a monthly benefit. It makes life less complicated – a very good thing.

There are specialists in long-term care insurance – make sure you use one! I've got a recommendation for you in the Resources section.

## Develop a Plan

Talk to your parents, evaluate their needs, and listen to their preferences. Develop a thoughtful plan for the time that they will need more care. Do they want to live near one of their children? Will they need to move in order to do that? Will they remain at home no matter what?

All these things will factor into the type and amount of long-term care insurance they purchase. It will factor into how they get care and how much it will cost.

Ultimately, it will be up to the person who is responsible for their care to make the final decision. If it stresses you to travel 2000 miles every two months to check on them, your preference that they live near you will loom large in the decision. If you already live next door, their wishes may be easier to meet.

Do your homework on the current cost of care at local facilities near your parents. Find out the daily cost of nursing care (the full cost, including extras) and the daily cost of assisted living. Call a few home health agencies and find out the hourly rate and minimum amount of hours for an aide to attend to an elderly person. You will be glad you got real numbers before you start to calculate how much LTC insurance your parents will need. I have shared some more tips to help you calculate in the Resources section.

# Implement

Choose your coverage and select a plan. Buy it now! It doesn't matter what age your parents are; buy it now. It can only get more expensive and they will only have less money. Don't stress about this – just buy what they can afford. We purchased my mom's plan when she was 80. She didn't need it until age 92. We received as much in the first two years of receiving benefits as we paid in premiums over ten years. It was a great investment.

Policies have several ways that you can pay the premium. It really saves a bundle to pay it annually, rather than monthly or quarterly. Do that if you can.

You can pay premiums until you need the benefit. Alternatively, some companies allow you to pay it all ahead and stop at age 65, or to prepay the full premium in the first ten years of the policy. If you can find a policy that allows you to prepay in larger amounts and stop at a certain age or year, I would recommend that you go for that option. Your parents will likely have fewer funds the older they get. If they can pay the premiums when they have more resources available, they can breathe easier during their later years.

But seriously, don't postpone this one! If you do nothing else that I suggest, *do this*! Buy as much as your parents' funds can support. And while you're at it, buy a long-term care policy for yourself too. You'll have saved Grace, your mom, your dad, your pocketbook, and your marbles.

------------------------------------

*Possibly the biggest myth in eldercare today is that Medicare will pay for long-term care like assisted living or long-term skilled nursing care. Long-term care insurance can help cover these costs.*

------------------------------------

"Who's going to pay for my long-term care?"

## Chapter 6

# Finding a Place to Park Them

Housing your elders is a multi-faceted decision. What works now may not work next month or next year. We will look at a range of options so that you can know the full spectrum of choices and the terminology that goes with them.

## Home Sweet Home

Staying at home is usually the first choice of our elders. They love their stuff and they have tons of it. They like being in the familiar; we all do.

It is often the least expensive option as well. Many older homeowners have no mortgage, and other than property taxes and upkeep, have very little in housing expenses.

Evaluating this option means looking at the home through a different set of lenses (not the ones you have always used to see your parents' home – put on the horned-rimmed ones!). Does it have stairs? Is there a bedroom on the main floor that could be used if needed, either full time or temporarily after a hospital stay? Is there a bathroom on the main floor? Is the only access to laundry in the basement? Are the doors wide enough for a walker or a wheelchair? Is the tub or shower safe to get into and out of for an elderly person? Does the front or back entrance have stairs? Is there a railing for assistance? Is the flooring slippery or uneven?

Your parents may be fine at home now. For the future, you will need to assess its comfort and safety for them as they age. You may develop a plan to retrofit the house with features that allow them to stay there safely if they have a handicap or are unable to move independently.

An important point to consider about old folks and moving – they don't go well together. Moving is a big deal for seniors and requires a lot of emotional and cognitive capital from them that they may not be able to recover. Evaluating their options and making a move earlier than later makes for a much better outcome.

If their current home doesn't work well for their later years, then there are a number of other living arrangements that you could consider, depending on your parents' needs.

## Independent Living/Active Living

This term generally refers to living arrangements that resemble an individual home, but are located in a community meant for seniors or retirees. These communities often incorporate social activities, recreation options, and building maintenance. It offers seniors who can live independently the added benefit of group activities and recreational options that they would not have in a single household. These communities handle property upkeep and maintenance and relieve older folks of some of the physical work that can prove more difficult and complicated as they age. Plus, it takes maintenance and upkeep off your "honey-child to-do list."

Most independent living options do not provide medical care or assistance with services. They may offer monthly blood pressure checks or weekly trips to the grocery store or pharmacy in a bus or van. But home health aides, medication reminders, and other needs for care usually cannot be accommodated in this environment.

## Assisted Living

When your parents need to take that first step into elevated care, it usually means moving into assisted living. The range of services available through assisted living is quite broad. Options can include simple services like providing meals or reminders to take medication. They can also ramp up to assistance with any number of ADLs like bathing, dressing, and incontinence care. Most often, you pay for the range of services that you need. More care, more cost.

If your parents are bluffing about eating, taking their medications, and cleaning their clothes, they need assisted living care.

Assisted living facilities may be stand-alone or they may be associated with a skilled nursing care facility. This is worth an evaluation when you are comparing your parents' needs to what is being offered. If your parent can move from minimal assistance to nursing care in the same facility or campus, it means they will not have to move as they age. That's a good thing!

If your parent just needs a few services like meals, laundry, and medication reminders, they may be perfect candidates for a stand-alone assisted living facility for years. Many assisted living residences offer apartment-type units that will allow your parents to remain quite independent (even cooking their own meals if they choose).

As you might expect, the cost range for assisted living is huge. It varies by geography, level of care, and condition of the residence. You will want to visit several in your quest for the perfect spot for your parents. Remember that they did lots of apartment hunting with you in your teens and twenties!

One recommendation: you get the best deal when you get the services bundled. Some facilities will offer a great rate on a room or apartment but charge for *every little thing your parent needs*. For example, phones, meals, activities, laundry, pets, parking, and care services can all be charged as add-ons to your parents' monthly costs. Find the facility that offers the most in one bundle, and you will usually be getting the better deal.

Some assisted living facilities offer 24-hour nursing on site. They may have registered nurses on duty at all times or just during the regular work day (8 AM to 5 PM), with licensed practical nurses working at night and on weekends. This is a wonderful benefit. It means your parents can get care where they live, rather than having to haul them off to the doctor for every little complaint or medical need. And you don't have to get in your jalopy and take them!

There are assisted living residences that operate in regular homes. Often these have a caretaker who either resides there with the residents or who stays with them for extended periods. This is a nice option if your parent likes the feeling of being at home but needs an elevated level of care with meals and other assistance with ADLs.

# Rehabilitation Facilities

These facilities are temporary care residences where folks go when they leave the hospital but can't care for themselves alone at home while they recover. Medicare usually pays for a qualifying stay at a rehab facility for 20 days (sometimes longer with a copay, depending on need).

Rehab facilities are often associated with skilled nursing care facilities; they either operate alongside them or as a separate division of the same organization.

If your parent is sent to a rehab facility, you can usually select the one you prefer. Visit several in the 2-3 days prior to your loved one being released from the hospital. Make sure the facility takes your parent's insurance and will work with you on specific care needs and preferences. The social workers at the hospital can give you a list of facilities to check out. Just remember, the hospital will call you about an hour ahead of your parent's discharge and tell you that they are putting your parent out on the front walk. You'll want to have your selection made by then!

Schedule a care conference for the first week that your parent is in the rehab facility. Treat this facility as you would the hospital – set your expectations of care and ask for regular updates on your loved one's progress. Your parent still needs an advocate – even if they are only there temporarily.

Remember in the long-term care insurance section, I mentioned the bed reservation benefit? If they have this benefit, your parent's LTC plan will pay to help keep their regular residence funded while they are recuperating in a rehab facility.

# Skilled Nursing Facilities

These are what many refer to as nursing homes. They provide extensive care for the elderly when they are not capable of caring for themselves.

Unlike assisted living, skilled nursing services are usually bundled, although every facility is different. The charges can be calculated on a daily or monthly basis – most often for a shared room, with an upcharge for a private room.

A skilled nursing facility is the most expensive care option and also requires the most research. The facilities vary widely in their cleanliness, attentiveness to patients, and nurse-to-patient ratio. Visits to these facilities are imperative – go at unusual times (like weekends or evenings) and ask for a tour. Observe what the patients are doing and how well their personal appearance is maintained. Does it smell clean? Listen for obnoxious beeping and other repetitive sounds. How does it feel? Does the place have an air of happiness and contentment?

Where is the nursing station located? How many nurses do they have on staff at any given time? How many are Registered Nurses (RNs), how many are Licensed Practical Nurses (LPNs) or Licensed Vocational Nurses (LVNs)? RNs have a higher level of education and certification than LPNs and LVNs, while LPNs and LVNs can perform routine care under the supervision of an RN.

How many aides do they have? In general, more aides mean more care.

Can the staff hear patients from the nursing station? Is there a paging system if the patient falls or needs help? Is there a doctor on staff or do geriatric specialists visit the facility regularly? Is there a physical therapy room at the facility? Do they have speech, occupational, and physical therapists on staff?

Ask how often the patients are bathed, showered, or changed? What is the daily routine? Is there an activity director? Do they accept input on activities? What about meals? Are they served at specific times in a dining room or are they taken to the patient's room?

How are medications handled? Who does the ordering? Who manages the patient's medication chart? How are vital signs measured and how often?

How is the family incorporated into the patient's care? Does the facility encourage regularly scheduled care conferences between family members and caregivers?

Some facilities have a chapel and chaplain services are offered. Some have a garden or courtyard where patients can sit outside. Many offer a beauty salon/barber shop on-site. Some even have a general store where residents can purchase sundries, cards, and little extras like ice cream!

A great resource for comparing average costs for eldercare by state can be found on the website for Genworth Insurance. See the Resources section at the end of the book.

## Your House

Well, there's always your house.

In times past, extended families lived together in relative harmony. The older folks took care of the little ones. When the older family members needed care, the younger ones provided it. We still do that in our society, although much less often than in the past. With two working spouses, it is often difficult to give the elders the extensive care they sometimes need. However, many families find it cost-effective and comforting to have their parents move into their home when they are no longer willing or able to live independently.

Many of the same concerns apply to your home as they do to your parents' (as we learned in the Home Sweet Home section above). Houses need to be fitted or retrofit for things like walkers, wheelchairs, and hospital beds. Home health aides can be employed to supplement care that cannot be provided by relatives.

Keeping your parents in your house can be a mixed blessing. In the "pros" column, the costs can be much lower when you compare the costs of your home to a residence facility. Keeping them at home also makes it easier for you to interact with them, know their care needs, and manage their business. After all, they live right there with you.

In the "cons" column, the emotional and privacy costs can be higher if they are living in your space 24/7. You might start to feel overwhelmed with their requests and needs; you could feel that you don't have a place to "get away or retreat" from the pressures of caretaking. Caring for elders can be physically demanding as well. If you don't have the strength or stamina to provide for their physical care, it might be difficult to have them staying in your home.

This is a personal choice. If you take this route, make sure all the people involved have stated their preferences, set ground rules, and have open lines of communication *before* you have them move in with you. If you don't, expect to lose lots of hair – you will be pulling some amount of it out each day.

## Making A Selection

"Different strokes for different folks" is the phrase that comes to mind here. The most important thing to remember is that you need to match your parents' care needs, budget, and comfort levels with their living arrangements. The one factor that I want you to consider here as you develop a plan is this: *moving a parent earlier in life is better than later.* Moving is stressful, especially for elders. They'll need to make new friends, become comfortable in their surroundings, and settle into a new routine. This all works out better when they have the physical stamina and mental acuity to handle the change. Saying "better late than never" doesn't work here. It's more like, "better never than late."

------------------------------------

*Have a candid discussion with your parents about where they would like to live as they age. Evaluate their needs, their budget, and your ability to participate in their care at that location. If your parents need moving, remember earlier is much better than later.*

------------------------------------

# Chapter 7

# Medicare Made Simple (Yeah, Right!)

**Y**ou don't have to be a dummy to get confused by Medicare. I think the whole program was made to act like a brainteaser puzzle for the elderly and their caretakers. It's complicated, confusing, and illogical. However, if you start with this premise, you'll do fine. Oh, and add in grateful – it is also a wonderful thing. Kind of like our parents...

If you are going to effectively assess what your parents' medical situation is, what care needs they have and how best to handle them, you are going to need to understand the System. The System includes Medicare, how it works, what is missing from current eldercare medicine, what kinds of assistance are available to take care of their needs, and what that assistance might cost.

In this section, I will explain the basics of how Medicare coverage works. This is not an advanced course. It is not a dictionary of terms. Just some cheat-sheet notes to help you navigate the system smartly. Well, maybe that's going a bit too far, but I promise this will indeed help.

## Medicare Enrollment

Medicare coverage usually starts when you turn 65 years old. If a person is disabled or has End-Stage Renal Disease, they can apply to get Medicare prior to age 65. Without those two exceptions, there is a 7-month initial enrollment period for Medicare, starting the three months before you turn 65. If you don't enroll during this period, there will likely be penalties in your Part B premium. I'll explain that next – just remember enrolling during this time window is imperative. You enroll by visiting the Social Security website or by going to your local Social Security office. You can also call Social Security's toll-free number. See the Resources section for complete details.

Besides the initial enrollment period, there is a general enrollment period that runs from January 1 – March 31 of each year. If you enroll during this period, your coverage would begin on July 1 of that year. If you sign up during the general enrollment period, but after your initial seven-month enrollment period, there will likely be penalties that add costs to your premium.

## Medicare Coverage

Medicare is both hospital insurance and medical insurance. Medicare Part A is hospital insurance, while Medicare Part B is medical insurance. Part A covers inpatient hospital care, skilled nursing facilities (not long-term care), and some home health care. Part A includes the Medicare-covered hospice costs as well. If you have worked in a job and paid FICA taxes for 10 years or more, you will likely receive Part A with no additional premium.

Medicare Part B covers medical care outside of a hospital – in doctors' offices, in outpatient facilities, in labs as well as the services of therapists. It also covers some home health care. The premium for Part B is charged monthly. It usually is deducted from the monthly Social Security payment. As of 2015, the Part B premium was $104.90. Part B premiums may be higher if your parents have a higher income. Medical services have to be deemed "covered" and "medically necessary" to be covered by Part B, unless the service is considered preventive care. Supplemental insurance policies usually will not cover any services or therapy that Medicare does not cover.

With Part A, Medicare covers hospital stays less a deductible for the first 60 days (the deductible was $1260 in 2015). There is a coinsurance payment per day for days 61-90 ($315 in 2015). If more than 90 days are required, you can use lifetime reserve days (you have 60 to spend in your lifetime), but you'll pay daily coinsurance ($630 in 2015). Skilled nursing facilities have their own requirements to be covered by Medicare but, generally, if the stay qualifies, they are covered in full for 20 days, then you pay a daily coinsurance up to 100 days.

Hospice care is covered by Part A as well. Included in hospice care is a team consisting of a doctor, nurses, counselors, social workers, therapists, and aides. Some hospice groups have trained volunteers as well. Medicare pays for the services of this team while the patient is terminally ill, as certified by your physician. They do not pay for any treatments intended to cure a terminal illness. They also do not pay for room and board at an inpatient hospice facility or long-term care facility. This is noteworthy because, if your parent becomes so ill that they can no longer stay at home and be cared for there, Medicare will generally not pay for the room and board part of a stay as an inpatient (some exceptions exist for respite care or pain/symptom management). Room and board for inpatient stays can cost in the range of $200-250 per day. Remember the LTC insurance coverage for hospice care? Well, it pays for the room and board costs.

With Medicare Part B, you also pay an annual deductible. In 2015, it was $147 a year. Some supplemental insurance policies cover this deductible and some do not. After the deductible, Medicare generally covers 80% of the "approved" cost of a covered service. "Approved" costs are what Medicare determines that a service or procedure should cost. The patient is responsible for the remaining 20% of the "approved cost" plus any excess charges. Excess charges are those amounts over the approved Medicare cost that providers are allowed to charge (but only if your provider does not accept Medicare assignment). Providers cannot charge over the approved Medicare cost if they are to continue to be an approved Medicare provider (or in industry terms, take Medicare "assignment"). Some supplemental insurance policies pay for excess charges and some don't. Check your parents' policy.

## Medicare Plans

There are two broad categories of Medicare plans. One is called "Original Medicare" and the other is referred to as "Medicare Advantage." Original Medicare is what most folks think of when they refer to Medicare. Although there are different types of plans offered in this category, they all allow the patient to go to any doctor, hospital, or medical provider who accepts Medicare. Payments are made to the providers at a certain percentage of "approved" costs and the patient (or supplemental insurer) is expected to pay the remainder.

Medicare Advantage plans (previously called Medicare Part C) act more like HMO or PPO plans than traditional medical insurance. They usually allow you to use only providers in their network; but they generally cover more for a lower cost. With Medicare Advantage plans, a private insurance company contracts with Medicare to provide both Part A and Part B services to the patient. There is usually a monthly premium in addition to the Part B premium, but it can be lower than traditional supplementary plans. Some Medicare Advantage plans cover items like dental care and eye care that are not included in Original Medicare coverage. There are two drawbacks to these types of plans. One is the patient is generally limited to the care providers in that particular plan. This can be an issue when the patient has been seeing their providers for years. They may not want to change providers if theirs are not in the plan. The other drawback to Medicare Advantage plans: once you enroll in one, you generally cannot go back to

Original Medicare unless your insurance company stops offering that plan in your area. Buyer beware!

## Medicare Supplemental Insurance

If you have Original Medicare, a number of insurance companies offer supplemental insurance policies (they supplement what Medicare does not pay). These policies cover a spectrum of costs, from the annual deductibles to the patient coinsurance. There are preset plans that are the same across the country. An alphabetical letter, for example Plan N, differentiates plans. Each plan covers a different set of items that the patient is expected to pay out of pocket with Original Medicare. Some plans cover deductibles; some do not. Some plans cover overseas medical costs; some don't. A complete comparison of these supplemental plans can be found at the Medicare website. It is very thorough. Pricing varies by region of the country, state, and type of plan.

## What Medicare Does Not Cover

*WARNING – Medicare does not cover:*
- Long-term care (sometimes called custodial or nursing care)
- routine dental, eye, or foot care
- dentures

- hearing aids or hearing exams
- glasses or contacts.

If your parents have coverage through a retirement plan or a previous employer, they could still have coverage for vision, hearing, and dental care. This is worth checking on; these are always some of the most frequently used and most expensive types of care received by seniors. Also, some supplemental insurance policies offer discounts on these services, but you have to read up on their policies to know how to get them.

## Assess and Evaluate

Spend some time on this aspect of your parents' expenses. Compare how they use the medical system to what their coverage is; see if they match. Many times, seniors pay for a supplemental insurance plan that's more expensive and covers all charges, but they don't see a doctor frequently enough to justify the added expense. Some plans are less expensive but cover costs only after deductibles or copays. If your elders travel outside of the USA frequently, make sure their supplemental insurance covers overseas medical costs. Original Medicare does not.

If your parents' current physician and specialists are in the network of a Medicare Advantage plan, then it may be a good solution for them. However, the fact that you can't change back to Original Medicare outside very special circumstances seems a bit too risky for my taste.

## Low-Income Senior Assistance

States offer low-income senior assistance with Medicare deductibles and coinsurance payments. See the state Medicaid office in your parents' state of residence or find more info on qualifying income levels on the Medicare website. I would go into this more, but although Medicaid is a national program, it is administered on the state level and every state program is different.

## Think It's Simple Yet?

I give you this information with a big qualifier – the facts and figures are subject to change every year. Further, Medicare coverage can change as new legislation like the Affordable Care Act goes into effect. Check regularly for changes.

Understanding Medicare and the nuances of its coverage are overwhelming to most folks. Simplicity and Medicare do not go hand in hand.

However, knowing the basics and matching your parents' coverage to the way they use the health-care "system" can save much in the way of expenses and headaches over the long term. Simply put, this probably won't be your most favorite part of caretaking...

--------------------------------

*Knowing what Medicare does and does not cover is important in eldercare. Understanding how the program works will help you maximize benefits for your parents, minimize their own financial outlays, and plan for expenses that are not covered.*

--------------------------------

# Chapter 8
# This is Your Parent on Drugs...

Prescription medicine is a huge part of most seniors' lives. Managing it drives them crazy but also keeps them going. You will want to understand how prescription drug insurance works, just like you do Medicare, because it has just as much impact on their finances.

Prescription drug insurance coverage can be a part of your parents' medical insurance or it can be purchased separately.

If your loved one worked for a company and has retirement benefits, he or she may have prescription drug coverage already. Otherwise, they have to enroll in a plan and purchase it just like they would Medicare supplemental insurance.

Annual enrollment periods typically occur during the last few weeks of the year, and these periods are the only time that your parents can switch prescription drug coverage, if they desire. Like supplemental plans, the various plans offered in your parents' area can be found and compared on the Medicare website. See the Resources section.

Each prescription drug insurance plan (Rx plan) has their own network of pharmacies and a formulary of drugs that their plan covers. The plans charge a monthly premium and most require the patient to pay a deductible each year before they will begin to cover prescription costs. The maximum deductible usually increases every year, but it varies. Check with each Rx plan for specifics. Note that some plans have no deductible.

Like with Medicare, states offer assistance with medication costs and deductibles to low-income seniors. Contact the state's Medicaid office for details. Again, Medicaid programs are different in every state.

You will want to compare the pharmacy network in each plan to what's actually available in your parents' location and where your parents prefer to shop. For example, if the Rx plan offers the best prices at a certain store, you will want to make sure your parents can get to that store easily. If your loved ones have a favorite neighborhood pharmacy, you'll want to confirm that pharmacy is in-network on the plan.

You will also want to get a list of your parents' prescription medications and compare them to the formulary covered by each plan. A formulary is the list of prescription medication covered by the Rx plan. Comparing their medications to the formulary confirms that your parents can actually get coverage for the drugs that they need. Formularies are arranged in tiers. They may have 4 or 5 tiers of drugs. Generally, the lower tiers cost less than the upper tiers. There may be a cheaper generic that falls in tier one that can replace the brand name drug in tier three, for example.

Most seniors expect that their Rx plan will cover a drug if their doctor writes a prescription for it. This is not always the case. To find out for sure, check the formulary of the Rx plan (online, in the booklet that was sent with the plan, or through the plan's customer service line). You can also ask the pharmacy to check for you.

Mail order pharmacies are associated with many of the Rx plans available. I have a love/hate relationship with these mail order pharmacies. They can save your parents huge amounts of money over a traditional retail pharmacy, but they can drive you to drink with trying to negotiate the system (and they are all different). I've dealt with great mail order pharmacies and I've dealt with some stinky ones too. But they all get 90 day supplies of prescriptions to your parents more cheaply and more conveniently than dealing with retail pharmacies who usually limit the fill to 30 days' worth of drugs. Of course, these advantages only apply to routine prescriptions of maintenance medicines. It almost always pays to use retail pharmacies for occasional antibiotics or medicines prescribed for short-term conditions.

Speaking of getting a list of medications that your parents take, you will want to have an updated list in your files for multiple purposes. If it didn't change so much when folks get older, I'd suggest a tattoo of the list since you'll need it so often. When your parents go to a new doctor (or visit a current doctor that they see infrequently), the doctor's office will want a list of their medications and allergies. Don't forget to include their vitamin and herbal supplements. When your folks are getting ready for a medical procedure, such as cataract surgery or a colonoscopy, the facility will want a copy of their current medications and allergies too.

If you move them to a new care facility, the facility will want a list of medications as well as a summary of their medical history. It pays to keep this list where you can get to it quickly and easily. In fact, keep a copy in your wallet and put one in your parents' wallets too (they won't be able to find it, but searching gives them something to do while you are filling out the medical forms for them at the doctor's office).

The number and type of medications that your parents use often increases with age. You will have to check periodically to remain current with their list.

If your parent needs diabetic supplies, nebulizer treatments, or special medical supplies, they will generally need a certificate of medical necessity written by their doctor before Medicare or supplemental insurance will pay for them. Check with the doctor. Ask the doctor to write the certificate if in doubt. It can't hurt to have it.

If your parent has a language barrier or if they have some cognitive impairment, it is best to have someone go with them to the pharmacy so that they come away with what they need and the instructions necessary to use the medication/item properly. Imagine them coming home with a stool softener when they needed a cough suppressant. It probably won't help their immediate symptoms and you'll need to make another trip anyway. Having a companion accompany your elders keeps them safer and helps to avoid multiple trips out and back as well. The same goes for phone calls to mail order pharmacies – join in the conversation via conference or 3-way calling. By the way – one of the best features on my phone for eldercare is the 3-way calling function. It works great when you are not physically near your parents to accomplish all kinds of business!

Fair Warning: You may want to use drugs recreationally after you deal with your parents' Rx insurance (like their prescriptions have been sent to your address for the 5th time after confirming that your parents' delivery address is 2000 miles away in Florida). It's ok. We all have that feeling. Try a latte.

---

*Prescription drug insurance is separate from medical insurance. The same insurer may carry them but they are not the same thing. Know what medications and supplements your parents take and keep a list of them handy. When you are evaluating Rx insurance, it is important to compare deductibles, identify which pharmacies are in the network, and whether a mail order program is available – in addition to comparing medication prices.*

---

# Chapter 9
# The Missing Link

The number of doctors and care professionals that your parents see goes up in an inverse proportion to the amount of coordination of that care that is being done. In other words, they are seeing more care providers, but you can bet that none of them knows the whole story about your parents' care. Having more providers means each one controls a smaller piece of the pie, and it's rare if anyone looks at more than their slice.

For example, the cardiologist prescribes a blood thinner, which requires a dietary regimen that eliminates many green leafy vegetables and requires careful monitoring of their blood-clotting factor. The primary care doctor hears your mom say that she hates taking the huge horse pills for calcium every day. She suggests to your mom that she eat more green leafy (calcium-rich) vegetables instead. The dentist wants to do some gum surgery on your mom and schedules it for next week. Drum roll...

If all three are not coordinating (and your mom does not understand the ramifications of all this care and how her prescriptions affect her), your mom will be bleeding too much during gum surgery due to the blood thinning medication, and she will be cutting down on the effectiveness of the blood thinner by eating the vitamin K-rich veggies.

The same goes for the gynecologist who prescribes estrogen hormone cream and the breast oncologist who would scream if she knew your mom was taking estrogen therapy (even localized in a cream).

This is the missing link in elder medical care: the coordination.

Enter YOU! – Stage Left!

You have to be the advocate and the coordinator. You will need to remind your parents to be completely thorough and clear about their medications and therapies to all care providers. They (or you) will need to ask about how one therapy affects another, how one medication can be affected by a new prescription or proposed procedure. Chapter 12 (the "no sale look" chapter) has a good tool to help with this.

Better yet, ask that the providers talk to one another or at least coordinate care at pre-set intervals (like semi-annually). Radical, I know! But your parents' health status can change suddenly; at least you will have started the conversation.

The amount of advocacy needed by your parents increases with their age and care needs. This can become the biggest consumer of your time. Getting comfortable as an advocate, knowing when to step in and who to contact for help will be some of the best investments you can make in eldercare.

You will usually find one real gem in your parents' health care system that you can lean on for help. This may be their primary care physician, it may be the head nurse at their care facility, or it may be your home health aide. This person can help you advocate for your parents' best care. Organize a search party and go find this person (or just ask around and see who can help).

It would be nice to imagine a giant circle of care providers with your parents in the middle, all singing Kumbaya. In the real world, you almost need to light a fire under their you-know-whats before they'll even speak to one another. But, be the nagging child here and advocate for the "coordination" of your parents' care.

---------------------------------

*Coordinated care is an endangered species. Your elder needs an advocate to ensure good health care and services. Often, that advocate is you or one of your siblings. Advocacy is best handled with a strong, clear voice and a determined spirit.*

---------------------------------

# Chapter 10

# Hiring a Nanny

**R**emember this project from when your kids were little (this may be very recent for some of you)? You were stressed about getting a nanny or a sitter that would be responsible, fun, and have a good moral character. Well, ditto here.

Understanding home health care assistance is critical to managing care for your parents if they are not being cared for by a facility.

## Who provides care?

Home care aides are mostly found working for home care agencies. Some though, are independent contractors and work outside of an agency.

Agencies screen their caregivers and back up their services with licenses, bonding, and insurance. They have a large staff, usually, and can match a caregiver to the specific needs of your parents. Independent caregivers can be less expensive and more flexible in their hours and care minimums. Sometimes, independent caregivers can be more responsive to your parents' needs as well.

Most senior resource publications (commonly

called *blue books*) have information about home health care agencies. Blue books are often available for free in the waiting rooms of doctors' offices, clinics, and hospitals. You can also search for local home health care agencies on the Internet (and get reviews on them too). Don't forget to ask around your parents' circle of friends, even at their church or community groups, for the names and references of caregivers.

## What care do they provide?

They provide a range of services from cooking and light housekeeping to assistance with ADLs like bathing and dressing. They can be hired for companionship, as escorts on errands and for shopping, or for helping with elders who have dementia or some other cognitive impairment. They can also help with mobility issues.

If you can think of something that is basic to living a life (including maintaining your sanity), generally the home care agencies can help your parents with it.

## How do they work?

Well, first, you and your parents determine what they need help with and then you contact a home care provider. Get bids from several providers.

In general, the agencies charge in the range of $15-40 per hour, with a minimum number of hours required (like 3 or 4). Sometimes, the agencies will work with you if you need fewer than the minimum hours, but will charge more per hour in exchange. Home health aides (who handle more caregiving) generally cost more per hour than homemaker aides (who do more housekeeping). CNAs (certified nursing assistants) cost more than non-certified aides but offer more education and skills. You may not care about the skills as much as you care about their experience and fit with your parents' needs. A great resource for daily/monthly/annual costs by state can be found on the website for Genworth Insurance. See the Resources section for details. Their survey has the link to home health aide costs by state as well as assisted living and nursing care costs. While you're there, look into getting a quote on LTC insurance (I keep getting back to that, don't I?).

Negotiate! Get out your best wheeler/dealer hat and negotiate. Sometimes it will work and sometimes it won't. Ask for what you need, ask for their best deal and then negotiate. The agency will usually tell you what they can negotiate on and what they can't. You may be able to work out a weekly program of services or set up a minimum monthly usage that varies by week or by type of service needed. If you don't negotiate, you will definitely pay the premium cost for the services that your parent needs. Remember, money doesn't grow on trees!

## Who works for whom?

The important thing to remember: the caregiver works for your parents – not the other way around. The caregiver should be sensitive to the fact that they are in your parents' home, that they are providing a service that can be degrading or undignified, and that they should be careful to watch for nonverbal communication as well as verbal instructions. A good match is critical. *If it isn't a good match, get a new caregiver.* This isn't a marriage; it's a service!

------------------------------------

*When hiring home health services, it is most important to look for fit between your parents/elders and the person(s) providing the service. The providers will be coming into your parents' home, into their personal space and assisting in some very vulnerable situations. The providers must be sensitive to the situation as well as a good fit with your parents' personalities and cognitive abilities.*

------------------------------------

# Chapter 11

# Getting Ready to Host
# The Antiques Road Show™ *

Remember that I told you your parents can't bluff about rubble? Well, there will be foothills, if not mountains, of stuff your parents have collected over the years. These are treasures to them and they will need to be "treasure chested" by you, either now or later.

Here are some suggestions for whittling away at the rubble, stuff, treasures, or whatever you call it. You have three choices: whittle away now, shortly before they move (assuming a move in the future), or during a move – a decision you'll want to make with your elders. But, be forewarned, this takes blood, sweat, and tears (well, usually less blood than the other two).

When you visit your parents, go with large totes and big shopping bags. Grab a few items off the coffee table and bookshelf. Okay, maybe that won't work. So you should at least start observing which items that they might want to keep, which

---

* ANTIQUES ROADSHOW is a trademark of the BBC and is produced for PBS by WGBH under license from BBC Worldwide.

items might need to go to Goodwill or to some other charity, and which items are fit only for the big green dumpster in the alley of the nearest shopping center.

Then, you can begin to shoplift during each visit. Just kidding! Or not!

## ID, Tag, and Segregate

Start with heirlooms. Ask your parents to tell you about them. The stories alone will be worth your time!

Get clear, permanent, adhesive labels at your local office supply store. Write a summary of the story of how and when the heirloom was acquired on the adhesive label. Attach it to the back or underside of the item. This prevents you from forgetting why it is an heirloom and preserves the story for future generations. This is great for furniture, keepsakes, and valuable collections. It's also great for family photos, and answering questions like, "who is that old geezer whose picture is in the hallway?"

Move on to furniture. Identify which items might want to be kept in the family and who your parents want to receive each item (or who has dibs on it). Mark this information on an adhesive label and stick it to the back of the furniture item.

This will help when it comes time to divide up the "antiques."

The dining room hutch, the guest bedroom, the basement, the garage, the tool shed, the barn – all are great repositories of rubble. Don't forget to go through closets and drawers. Your parents may want to "lighten the load" but just haven't had the initiative or the impetus to start. They may be grateful for your help with this process.

Usually there are three to five categories for stuff. I like to use colored dots (grab these from the office supply store as well) to categorize the items.

- Items that your parents want to keep with them no matter what (clothes, furniture, personal keepsakes, photos, basic personal items)
- Items that will go to family members (each person gets a different colored dot!)
- Items that can be sold at an estate sale or garage sale
- Items to donate to charity
- Items to throw away

## Be Bold!

This is not a time to be timid or indecisive! Make a decision about each item. Put it in one of those categories. The old rule always applies – if you haven't used it in a year, you won't use it – so get rid of it!

If you don't know about an item, put it in a pile to deal with later. But, warning, don't do this with too much or you'll want to pull your hair out when 'later' finally comes.

## Stages

Just like there are stages of grief, there are stages of rubble definition and dissemination. Your parents may want to do an initial wave now; then again if they move to another location, and again after they've been in the retirement place for a few months. Don't think if you've done this once, you're finished. Like an onion, there are going to be more layers to peel.

And, like exercise, the most important part is to just get started!

------------------------------------

*Paring down your parents' belongings is not a job for the faint-hearted. It can take several pass-throughs to sort, label, and distribute all of them. You might complete this in one big effort, but it might take more than a few moves to finish it. The important point is to start. Don't postpone this task. It is best done as a project, partnering with your parents.*

------------------------------------

# Chapter 12

# The "No Sale" Look and The "Huh?" Expression

**D**o you remember the old cash registers that had No Sale buttons that just opened the drawer and didn't do any calculations? Well, your parents also have that button.

As they get older, you will explain things to them that seem relatively straightforward and you will get a look from them that says No Sale. You may even get the guttural "huh?". It means that they totally missed the relevance of your explanation.

This brings up the quandary of how to get them to ask the right questions at the doctors' offices, how to make sure they carry forward any instructions that they have received (from any source), and how to get them to remember what they should tell you about their health, finances, or other important information.

They should begin carrying a journal, a notepad, or a planner where they can keep questions, answers, important dates, details, or appointments. If they are tech-savvy, they could do this on a tablet or computer. Computerized schedules and to-do lists can be shared by you and your parents (how handy!).

Ideally, the journal, planner or whatever will have sections – Medical, Home, Business, and Family tabs plus any other categories you think are important for them to track separately. **Medical** should have a place to record questions that they come up with between doctor visits, observations about their health that they want to pass along to a care provider, appointment reminders, reminders to refill/reorder prescriptions, and other notes pertinent to medical care.

The **Home** section will have reminders of when to do maintenance, a repair log, or notes about future shopping trips (like get a light bulb for Aunt Bessie's old lamp). You could also include info about what batteries go with which electronics or fixtures, reminders for when to replace certain items like filters, or when the renter's insurance renews each year.

**Business** will have information about business conducted or notes about a conversation in which promises were made for future follow-up. This section could remind them about annual meetings with financial advisors, magazine and newspaper renewals (you know your parents are tempted to renew early when they get notices every five minutes), or due dates for insurance premiums. It could remind them where important paperwork or keepsakes are stored.

**Family** will have important dates to remember – like the biannual family reunion on Memorial Day weekend or Mary's graduation next May. It could have a place for recollections that they want to share with grandchildren on their next visit or notes about a treasured keepsake that they want to pass on to a favorite nephew when he comes to town.

I know what you are thinking… "there is *no way* that my parent will keep a journal like that!" Well, maybe not, but what if they did? What if you showed them how easily they could make it work and how wonderful the benefits of keeping it would be? They don't have to keep it on paper either, as I said earlier; it can be kept on a computer or electronic device as well.

If you start them on this early in their aging process, using a journal will become a habit and eventually, part of their routine. When they get into this routine at age 65 or 70, they will still be in the habit at age 80. That's what you want to encourage – behaviors that enhance and support the aging process. Start now, rather than leaving it to later when they will not or cannot take up a new habit. It gives you and your parents tools for their journey. You need all the tools you can get in your bag.

If you didn't get to this in time for your parents to be able to do it, you may want to maintain their journal yourself – to both help them and help yourself keep all the info together and have a place of reference.

Whoever does the journal – it pays to be organized. Payment comes in coins of sanity; think about keeping your marbles in the bag.

You will thank me the next time you ask them (for the 4th time) if they remembered to get a date for their skin cancer follow-up so that you could work it around your next business trip and get a "huh?" combined with a No Sale look.

------------------------------------

*Helping your parent organize and keep track of "to-do" items is a task worth the time invested. If you don't live with your elders, you will especially appreciate tools that keep track of medical appointments, task reminders, and other items requiring your attention.*

------------------------------------

"But, Mom, working your new cell phone
is easy!"

# Chapter 13

# Sibling Rivalry

Remember when you wanted to be the one getting the most attention from your parents? Well, it works the opposite way as they get older. Most siblings jockey for being the one who gets the least amount of attention (or calls) from the elders. And, as it was when you were growing up, the need for attention may vary, but the way it actually gets divvied up is rarely equal or fair.

This chapter addresses evaluating how each family member can help shoulder the burden of your parents' eldercare.

## Shares and Votes

Who gets the most say in your folks' care and who gets veto powers? The most obvious way to distribute the voting shares is the distance factor. Those who live closest get the most amount of say because they will likely be the ones that provide the most care. If that is not the case in your family, determine who does the most for your parents. That party should get the biggest say (or vote) in their care. Have this discussion now and be candid about what you can/can't do and will/won't do.

## Proximity and Task Assignments

Do not assume that the family member living closest should do everything! Decide what needs to be done and who would be the best person for that job.

Examples of jobs that can be spread among family members include:

- Paying bills and handling money
- Going to doctor visits and medical procedures
- Regular shopping for groceries or household items
- Maintenance of the home and vehicles
- Handling legal work and taxes
- Sorting and disseminating the rubble
- Medications (ordering and purchasing)
- Medication reminders
- One time or infrequent tasks (like ordering hearing aids, glasses, or clothes-shopping)

If one family member cannot participate in a task, they might be able to provide the funds to hire someone to do that task.

Out-of-towners can handle bill payment and legal work more easily than they can regular errands and doctor visits. In fact, with the Internet, remote or online bill payment is easy. Most utility bills, rental payments, insurance, and banking can all be managed remotely now with little effort. They can also schedule infrequent tasks for when they visit the elders. In-towners can spread out the tasks that require being physically present, like doctor visits and weekly shopping trips. Plus, you and your siblings will each have different skill sets that will help narrow down what responsibilities are best handled by whom (unless you are all furniture movers like Brothers & Sisters Moving Co).

Some medical procedures can be scheduled around family member visits as well. (Remember to take the journal/planner notes with you!)

## Open Communication

The most important factor is keeping open and honest communication between family members. If you feel that you are carrying the heaviest burden, speak up and figure out a way for the others to help. If you live out of town, offer to pay for a service or caregiver to give the local family members respite.

Play fair. Be thoughtful. Be compassionate. Talk frequently.

My brother and I treat this like a relay race. I do some parts of a task and hand off the rest to him to complete. He's local and I'm not, but we work as a team.

In the end, this is your family and you'll still have them when your parents have gone to glory.* Doing all you can to keep the heavy lifting spread out among the team will do wonders for these relationships now and in the future.

---

*Sharing the care is the take-away here. No one deserves to have all of the work of eldercare if there are other family members to share it. Respect is the most important part of working together as a family to care for your elders. Asking all the players involved to help share the work is imperative.*

---

(*A note here about glory: I was raised in the South where "going to glory" is a phrase commonly used to describe the time when someone passes away. I use it in the book to describe death and dying, not in a religious sense, but as a humorous, non-threatening way of dealing with death.)

## Chapter 14

# The Topic No One Wants to Discuss – Hospice

Who wants to talk about a terminal illness? You'd rather walk uphill both ways in a snowstorm, right? Well, I understand. In your dreams (and mine too), your parent goes to sleep in their Lazy Boy chair and doesn't wake up – at just the right time in their lives and without suffering.

Unfortunately, that only happens in the movies and, well, to my Aunt Rosie.

I'm going to prepare you for when the doctor calls and says, "we need to put your parent in hospice care." My husband and I both got that call on the same day, each for one of our parents. My mother, of course, had a revival and never actually entered hospice.

We'll take a breather from the humor here. This is emotionally hard – but don't forget to laugh when you are going through it. Humor will keep more of those marbles in your bag.

# First of all, what is hospice?

Hospice care is care given to an individual when a doctor has determined that they have less than six months to live. It is palliative care, designed to minimize pain and discomfort – not designed to cure illnesses or prolong life.

# Who provides hospice care?

There are many providers – some hospitals have a hospice group, some providers come from independent organizations, some are associated with religious organizations, and some are in nursing care facilities. It is your parents' choice who provides their hospice care. Usually, your doctor or hospital will give you information on hospice care options in your area.

Hospice care is provided to your parent on an as-needed basis, but you have access to care 24/7. Initially your hospice provider will do an assessment of what your parent's care needs are and will assign a manager for that care (usually a nurse) along with a team of aides and therapists. You will have contact information for the team should you have questions or if your elder's needs change quickly as well as a phone number for around-the-clock access.

# How long can a patient receive hospice care?

As long as the patient continues to be diagnosed with a terminal illness by a doctor, the patient can receive hospice services.

Medicare has a specific guideline (of course!). You can get covered care for two 90-day benefit periods, followed by an unlimited number of 60-day benefit periods (as long as the patient is recertified as having a terminal illness by a doctor). You can change hospice care providers once during a benefit period. Visit the Medicare website and search for hospice to get all the details.

If your parent recovers or has a renaissance while they are in hospice care, they can move out of it by cancelling the program.

# Where is hospice care provided?

In the setting that works best to care for your parent – usually at home, but it is also offered in nursing care facilities and in-patient hospice facilities too.

So what should you do first? Just like the other projects that we've discussed, research is imperative here.

# Evaluate

Find three or more hospice providers and interview them.

Ask these questions (and more that you'll have too):

- Is this hospice agency licensed and certified with the state?

- How many care providers will be assigned to your parent? Who are they?

- Will their hospice doctor work with your parent's doctor if your parent chooses that option?

- How often will the hospice doctor visit with your parent? Can you request an unplanned visit with the hospice doctor?

- Who is on the nursing team? Is the nurse that will be assigned to your parent an RN or a certified nurse practitioner? How often will the nurse visit?

- How many patients are assigned to each hospice nurse and/or care team?

- What providers make up the emotional support team? Social workers? Chaplains? How will you access them?

- What kind of aide services are provided and covered by Medicare?

- Do they have a trained team of volunteers? What services do these volunteers provide? Will they come and sit with your parent if requested? Will they drive one spouse to see the other spouse if the loved one in hospice is not at home?

- How quickly can your parent receive medical equipment that may become necessary – hospital bed, toilet chair, walker, oxygen, etc.?

- What happens if your parent can no longer be taken care of at home or in their current facility? Where would they go? Who pays for the care? Under what circumstances would the care cost become the responsibility of your parent? *This last question is very important!*

- What happens in the final days/hours of the patient's life? What should you expect to see in your parent (called "signs of active dying")? The hospice nurse, doctor, and social worker are all good sources of specifics on this topic. What services can you expect from the hospice provider as death nears?

- How long after death will the family have access to bereavement counseling and the care team? Does the facility offer classes that a surviving spouse or family member can attend? Are there support groups?

## Assess

What hospice provider is the best fit for your parent? Go with your gut on this one. This is a challenging time for families and you need good support from your providers during this part of the journey.

## Who pays for hospice care?

Generally, Medicare covers hospice care. It's covered under the Part A section of Medicare coverage. Even if a patient is covered under a Medicare Advantage program, they still receive hospice care benefits under the Original Medicare program. Go to the Medicare website, search for hospice; their explanation of hospice care coverage should be your go-to place for understanding, in general, what is covered. It also explains what deductibles and coinsurance requirements there are for hospice coverage.

# What does Medicare NOT cover in the hospice program?

- Any treatment that could be considered "curative" for the terminal illness

- Prescription drugs to "cure" the terminal illness

- Care that was not set up by or approved by the hospice team

- Room and board (at home, at a skilled nursing facility, or at an inpatient hospice facility). This is the most expensive part of hospice care and is NOT COVERED unless the patient is receiving respite care or is deemed to be in need of short-term pain and/or symptom management. Important note: this cost would be covered under the hospice care rider of their LTC insurance policy!

- Emergency room care, care at an inpatient facility, or ambulance services if they are related to the terminal illness.

- Any treatment for symptoms or care not related to a terminal illness (this care is handled by the regular medical insurance that your parent has).

Let me take a moment here and give you a bit of an overview on hospice care criteria, as it relates to Medicare coverage. Once your parent has been diagnosed with a terminal illness and has entered a hospice program, the care they receive is only *palliative*. It is not curative. For example, if your elder has cancer and they've decided against further treatment from radiation therapy or chemo-therapy, Medicare will not cover any more therapies that might be rendered to "cure" or mitigate their cancer. They also won't cover x-rays, diagnostic procedures, or any other care that might indicate how far the disease has progressed.

> Note: Short-term pain and/or symptom man-agement means (roughly) that the patient has two or more symptoms requiring interventions that cannot be managed outside of an acute care facility. Think of hospital-level care – this is acute care. Dying is not considered a reason for acute care (very insensitive, I know).

## What is Respite Care?

"Respite care" is made available when the primary caretaker of the terminally ill patient needs some time off. Medicare will pay for 5 days of respite care at a time (usually the patient is moved to an inpatient facility). Room and board is covered during respite care, but there may be a coinsurance requirement. Use respite care to get some rest! And don't feel guilty about it if you do.

## Your job

Again, your job will be to serve as your parent's advocate during the time that they are cared for by a hospice program. This role becomes even more important as they move closer to death and, perhaps, cannot effectively advocate on their own behalf. You can share this responsibility with the other parent, but don't expect this to be a time of clear and rational thought for the surviving spouse.

Make sure the hospice organization is following the wishes of your parent(s). Stay in touch with the nurse assigned to your family, as well as the emotional care team (the social worker or chaplain). Make sure that the hospice team is responsive. This is a critical time for active and rapid response. If your parent needs symptom management for pain or discomfort, you want the team to be responsive and attentive.

I recommend that you read *Final Gifts* by Maggie Callanan and Patricia Kelly. They give tremendous insight into understanding the intensely personal time that occurs differently for each of our family members as they approach death.

Facilitate any communication that your dying parent wants to have with you or other family members. Listen to them and observe their non-verbal communication too. Help them achieve peace, if you can.

Some of our best memories of my father-in-law are from this time in his life when he was sensitive, loving, and genuine in his desire to communicate with all of us as he approached the end. By being properly prepared, you can help facilitate a gentler transition for everyone.

Your goal should be to ensure that your parent is as comfortable and as peaceful as possible during this time. This process is an opportunity for more than just mourning or anger. Make it a time of healing and closure for yourself and your loved ones, as well as your parents. It is hard and there are no passes to get out of it.

------------------------------------

*Hospice care is for people who have been diagnosed with an illness or condition estimated to take their lives in six months or less. By that definition, time is short, emotions are raw, and palliative care is the goal. This can be a special time between elders and their families, especially if there is a good fit between the patient, the location of care, and the hospice care team.*

------------------------------------

# Chapter 15
# The Exit Ramp

Well, at some point, your parents will go to glory. They will exit stage right and move on to whatever comes next. I could tiptoe around about this but, really, why? Aren't we all mortal? Bottom line: when your parents pass on, you'll need to figure out what to do with their bodies.

So here goes...

First off, I know you don't want to think that costs have anything to do with this decision, but they do. There are huge cost differences between burial options, funeral arrangements, cremation, and other alternatives. The right decision is located at the intersection of your parents' religious preferences, their family heritage/culture, and their budget. That's a big intersection. I hope it doesn't turn out to be a roundabout!

## Body Donation

If your beliefs allow it, one alternative (and a good one in my opinion), is to give the body to science. Most of these programs do not cost anything to the family and it offers great societal benefits: education and the advancement of science. You simply pre-register with a university program or with your state's anatomical board. When your loved one passes away, a call is made to the organization and they retrieve the body. They usually keep the body for 1-3 years and then return the cremains (the official term for cremated remains) to the family. Find programs in your area by searching for "body donation" on the Internet.

## Cremation

The average cost of cremation at a crematory is $1500 to $4000, a little more at a funeral home. Urns to hold the cremains can range from $30 to $1400 (no, the $30 option is not a fancy zip lock bag; you can find simple urns for inexpensive amounts). There will be additional costs relative to transporting the body from the place of death to the crematory as well as costs for the memorial service. Embalming is not needed prior to cremation, and in fact, is money thrown away if you plan to cremate the body (this may seem crazy but you might be offered this option). You can use an independent crematory or go through a funeral home to access this service. Cremation is not a substitute for a funeral or memorial service. If you choose to have a service, there will be additional costs related to this.

# Funerals

The typical funeral with burial will cost on average between $7000 and $10,000. Funeral home services will run around $6000, while the cemetery plot with burial will average $2000. Caskets can range from just under $1000 to over $8000 (included in the funeral home estimate). Caskets can also be purchased online – do a search and maybe even save some money. The headstone and marker may run another $250-3000, depending on the size of the stone and type of granite or marble. Embalming, which can cost around $500, is optional, especially if you can have the burial shortly after death. Most funeral homes will have access to a crematory, if you decide to go that route.

This business is full of "extras," designed to nickel and dime you into the ground. Beware! There is a fee for every little service: the transfer of remains, limos, guest books, filing paperwork, use of facilities for visitation or for a service, motorcycle escorts to the cemetery, bulletin printing, and on and on.

But that's how it is. Funerals are expensive and you can be making very costly selections at a time when your mind is not honed in on bargains. It is very wise to research these costs prior to needing the service, when you can be objective about what services you want and what doesn't feel necessary.

Ultimately, these decisions will be made by your family based on what your parent's final wishes were, and on how you choose to honor your parent's life. Just remember to be careful here and keep your wits about you (having your marbles here is good!).

## Pre-Planning

The pre-planning that you should be doing is as follows:

- Talk to your parents about what they would like to do with their bodies after death. Have them write it into their will, if they choose.

- If body donation is their choice, contact a medical school, university, or the state anatomical board. Process the paperwork now so they will be prepared for the donation (in months or years).

- If cremation is their preferred alternative, decide if you want to use an independent crematory or go through a funeral home. Decide where the cremains will be held (in an urn, divided among family members, sprinkled at sea or in some other beloved place). Your parents may have very specific guidelines in mind, or they may leave it up to you and other family members.

- If they want to be buried, find out where. Have they already purchased the cemetery plot? If not, now is a good time to locate their favorite place and purchase the needed space. You may want to use a family cemetery or you may want to consider purchasing a group of plots for family members who want to be buried close to one another.

- "I don't want to talk about it" is not a valid response. Remember the only things certain about life are death and taxes. It *will* happen. The more you talk about it, the more choices you will all have. There will be less stress in the final decisions, plus you'll feel better during "the process" and afterwards too.

---

*Death is not a topic most of us want to discuss. It is, however, important that we talk with our parents about their wishes for what happens when they pass. Planning ahead saves in many areas: emotions, time, and money.*

---

# Chapter 16

# Dealing with the Remains

No, I don't mean the body. I mean all the THINGS! Remember the rubble! Well, you won't be able to forget it now because it will be there to trip you up (literally!).

Hopefully, you have done what I suggested in chapter 11 and put info on the back of keepsakes, shoplifted the unwanted stuff during each visit, and hidden your favorite items from the rest of the family. If you have, just make a pile for each person on the list of recipients, based on the wishes of your parent or the wishes of their heirs.

Here are some things to remember:

- China, silver, and crystal sets should each be kept as a set, unless heirs agree to split them. They lose much of their value outside of a set. Internet dealer sites can be a resource for assessing what they are worth (and they buy pieces too).

- Separate all items that are to be kept from the items that are going to be sold or donated. You'll be so glad you used those colored dots now! Evaluate whether you have the time and/or the fortitude to do the disposal of these items yourself. You may want to hire a local estate sale company to handle it, but they will take a large percentage of the receipts. There are charities that take items like furniture, bedding, housewares, and clothing for domestic abuse victims or homeless people starting over. They are usually very grateful for gently used items that elderly folks have. There are also antique mall vendors who specialize in the sort of things that fill most older folks' houses. If you decide to dispose of their rubble yourself, check on EBay, Craigslist, and other sites for values and current pricing. You don't want to undervalue your stuff, nor do you want to price it like a Rembrandt if it's not.

- Don't forget friends and relatives like to have mementos from their loved ones. Give them a little keepsake or let them select what holds the most sentimental value for them. These folks are often passed over or forgotten when it comes to the "stuff," but their love and attachment to your parents may be enormous.

- Clothes can be given to other family members if they would like to have them. Sometimes, certain clothing has lots of sentimental value. Whatever remains can be donated to a charity of your choice.

  I would like to make a plug for some of them. Dress for Success helps give professional attire to disadvantaged women who are trying to get back on their feet. They can use the clothes to go on interviews or at new jobs. The Resources section has more info on this.

  Other wonderful uses of clothing include homeless shelters, youth and runaway centers, or domestic violence shelters. They need good clothing and can usually put it to use immediately.

- Family photos – if someone is in the photo, send it to that person. They will likely be thrilled with the surprise and the memories associated with it. Otherwise, make sure you've written the names on the back of the photo before you put it away or pass it along.

- Unused toiletries can be donated to shelters. They always need these kinds of goods.

- Don't forget Fido! Hopefully, your parents have decided where Fido should go after they have passed away (and they've told both you and Fido's new owner). If not, family members may be willing to take pets. Don't forget other elderly folks living near your parents or down the hall at their care facility may have an attachment to Fido and want to adopt him/her.

This is tough work. After they pass, you may not be ready to deal with it. You may have the luxury of putting everything into storage or in your barn and dealing with it at your own pace. You may not.

Ask for help. Get the siblings together to tackle this as a project. You may have some wonderful laughs and great memories to revisit as you disseminate your parents' stuff. A cousin or other relative may be able to help as well. They probably won't have all the attachments to your parents' things that you have, and that can help you remain clear-headed.

There are services that do "rubble categorization and removal" for you (hint: don't look under this category in the Yellow Pages). Estate sale companies are the most common. The senior blue book directory in your area often lists these service companies. You'll still probably have to start the process though.

Don't forget to thank anyone who helps with this job. It is tough to do and should come with a reward (how about they take some of the rubble?).

---------------------------------

*This is tough work. Being organized, asking for assistance, hiring professionals, and staying focused on the task at hand will be the keys to accomplishing this work quickly and efficiently. Remember, folks who help care for your elders as well as extended family might like some personal keepsakes too.*

---------------------------------

# Chapter 17

# The Fat Lady is Just Getting Warmed Up!

**Y**our parent or relative just passed away. You are grieving, but can now take a deep breath. It's finally over. Well, don't breathe that sigh of relief quite yet – the fat lady is not singing! In fact, she's not even in the building.

There is still so much to do. All of the final paperwork and official notification of death looms before you. Cue the music: Addams Family theme song.

This isn't an exhaustive list, but it will get you started. And, believe me, you'll still be exhausted:

- Obtain a death certificate. You will want several official copies too. The funeral home may provide the original copy. You can also obtain the official documents from the Vital Records Department of the county where your loved one passed. Usually, they offer a discount for additional copies. Do your best estimate from this list and add 1-2 for you to keep in your files.

- Contact your parent's attorney. They will need to execute the will and/or handle any legal aspects of the estate.

- Go to the Social Security office. You're better off doing this in person and within the month of the death. Take a book, your iPad, and/or snacks – this can be a time-consumer. Remember the form you had your parent fill out that allowed you to represent them to Social Security? You will be glad you have it now!

  If a spouse survives your loved one, you will need to take the spouse, their marriage certificate, and the death certificate. The spouse will need a form of identification. If the widow(er) has survived a remarriage, take copies of the other marriage certificates and divorce decrees. The spouse will most likely be eligible for either his/her benefit or the deceased spouse's benefit, whichever one is higher. Check with the Social Security website but don't expect to be overwhelmed with useful info. For a moment (a very brief moment), you will feel amazed when the surviving spouse is handed the Social Security lump-sum death benefit of $255. It may even cover the cost of the death certificate copies or your travel expenses to Social Security if you don't live near an office! It may even have increased since I wrote this – oh come on, we can all dream!

- Social Security will notify Medicare – please note this does NOT work the other way around.

- Call the Medicare supplement insurance company that covered your parent (or the Medicare Advantage insurance company). Notify them of the death. Ask if they need a copy of the death certificate. Ask them to give you a new monthly payment amount for the remaining spouse, if that is applicable. Medicare will eventually notify them, but trust me, you don't want to try to get a refund on premiums paid after their death. Do you?

- Call any other insurance companies where your parent was insured. Life insurance, burial insurance, long-term care, auto, home, dental/vision/prescription – there are many types. Ask them if you can fax the death certificate to each (this saves on numbers of copies that you will have to order and pay for). Make sure you get the official date from them of when your loved one's files were closed or went inactive in their system. Ask about pro-rated refunds for partially covered months. Give them your address for any correspondence if a surviving spouse is not involved.

- Call the Veterans Administration if your parent was receiving benefit payments. They will probably want you to send or bring in a certified copy of the death certificate. Do this one quickly too – you don't want them to overpay and then force you to pay that money back! After all, you're dealing with former military and they know how to fight you for it.

- Call the county clerk's office for any county where your parent owned property, including vehicles. They will want a copy of the death certificate. Make sure you ask about transfer of ownership of this property into the name of the spouse or surviving heirs.

- Contact the bank and/or investment companies where your parent's funds are held. You should already be an authorized user and able to speak for your parent.

They will want to see a copy of the death certificate or may need an actual copy, depending on their policies. Pursue removing the deceased person's name from checks, credit cards, debit cards, authorized user lists, etc. Remember to cut up credit cards with the name of the deceased on them, but keep their Social Security and Medicare cards safely stored.

- Check your parent's credit card statement (if you haven't already been paying their bills) and look for any automatic payments that are withdrawn every month. Call each of these businesses and notify them of the death. The next steps will be determined by the nature of the charge and whether it needs to continue. Check the statements for the last 6-12 months to make sure you have spotted all the charges, including semi-annual and annual payments. Contact charities that are used to getting automatic donations too.

- Speaking of bills, make sure that you wait a sufficient time for all bills to clear before you close any accounts or disperse any remaining funds. It may take several months (sometimes up to a year) for medical bills to come in or for final refunds to be issued. You may have to call Medicare to make sure all claims have been paid in the months following the death – once your loved one goes inactive in the Medicare system, their claims may not automatically be paid. Medicare generally keeps your parent's file open for one year only. Be diligent here, claims will come out of the woodwork. Medicare plus insurance will handle most of them but you will be the *only* driver on this one – so put on your best driving cap.

- Contact any companies or organizations paying your parent a pension or annuity. They will likely want a copy of the death certificate. Determine when the last payment will be made and how it will be made. Don't close any accounts until you are sure that all final payments have been made. If a spouse survives, get a calculation of what the surviving spouse's benefit will be.

- Contact utility companies. Remember there can be several – phone, cell phone, electric, gas, cable, Internet provider, water, sewer, garbage, homeowner's association. Get the account transferred into either your name or the name of the surviving spouse. Don't forget to give them a new mailing address if appropriate.

- If they were renting, contact the owner or manager of their apartment, condo, or residence. Contact the mortgage company if they had a mortgage on their property, including a reverse mortgage.

- Make an appointment with your tax professional. Take copies of your parent's last tax return, wills, medical expenses, and income stubs. There are many items to discuss and they will be helpful members of the team going forward.

- Power of attorney does not apply after a person is deceased. Many of these tasks will have to be handled by the personal representative named in your loved one's will.

- Remember, take this one step at a time and budget the appropriate time to do this quickly and thoroughly. You will be very glad you did.

Now, can you hear the lady warming up?

------------------------------------

*There are many details to attend to after the death of a parent. You will have to commit some time and effort to these tasks. Attention to detail at this time will help make closing of their estate cleaner and easier.*

------------------------------------

# Chapter 18

# The Final Chapter

**H**ere's your big high five! You've done it! You've picked up this book. You've done research and dug up tons of information. You've thought about topics that you'd rather put on the back burner forever. And, you've made it! Congratulations! I am proud of you!

Now, go out and get started. Buy long-term care insurance, get the powers of attorney completed, delve into your parents' finances, start dealing with the rubble, begin to peel back the onion that is Medicare, and think ahead with all of it.

Trust me. It will wait for you. But, these things are not cheese and wine. They do not age well. They will become big and stinky if you ignore them.

But if you do these things, if you're proactive, resourceful, and organized now, you just might be able to get through this without losing your marbles. Maybe.

## In the end

When all is said and done, you will have stories. You will have memories and you will have endless topics to make you smile, tear up, or pull your hair out (probably all of the above).

This work makes for great stories, some almost unbelievable in their reality and truth.

Remember to keep your running shoes on, do your preparation, re-install your compassion bone, get your bossy voice out, and most importantly, laugh!

Love and hugs to you as you embark on this journey. I'll be waving to you from the shore! Bon Voyage!

# Resources for Eldercare Navigation

The following are sites and information that you can use to help with your individual eldercare experience. A note of caution – information on these subjects changes frequently and resources come and go. Please be aware that this is not an all-encompassing list, just a place to start.

**Legal Services**

Family attorneys are always best if you have one. They know their clients and have a history of working with them, allowing them to build more personalized documents.

Online legal forms are also helpful. One site that I find very helpful for do-it-yourself legal forms is USLegalForms.com. They have forms available by state, which is helpful and important. You pay for the forms by credit card and can receive them either electronically or in the mail. Other companies offer similar services – just search the Web for online legal forms.

## Senior Publications/Help Online

Most metropolitan areas have senior resource guides that you can pick up for free (often called the *blue book*). They list home health care agencies, available senior housing, transportation options, and medical provider information. They are usually filled with advertisements, but even those are helpful if you are looking for the product or service they are advertising. Pick up one at a nearby convenience store, restaurant, senior center, or hospital. They are usually on the free publication racks stationed near entrances and exits. Also, many doctors' offices have the blue books in their waiting rooms.

Some metro areas publish free magazines dedicated to senior issues. They often discuss topics of interest to folks over 55 as well as list local community events and activities.

The AARP publishes a magazine covering topics related to seniors. Swipe it off your parent's coffee table on your next visit. The AARP website is also chock full of helpful links. A great one is the "Caregiving Resource Center" – go to AARP.org and search for it. There are links to information about a wide range of topics from legal issues and money matters to health providers and caregiving support.

## State and Local Agencies on Aging

States and localities (if they are big enough) usually have a department or division dedicated to helping seniors and their caregivers. You can search your state government's website for their department on aging. The state site may direct you to local resources as well. For example, our eight-county area has teamed up to offer an agency on aging and a list of senior resources in the metro area covered by those counties. These departments mainly offer advice on where assistance is available, what resources are available and how to access them. Some offer ombudsman and advocacy services to elders using services in the community. They do not usually provide any direct assistance or eldercare services to individuals. They are great go-to resources for information and advocacy though!

## Community Organizations/Senior Centers

Most communities have some kind of senior program, whether it is an actual organization or just a group of folks who want to help seniors. Many senior centers take up residence in their own buildings, while others provide their services in community centers, town halls, and municipal buildings.

Some offer free or reduced cost transportation; some offer meals; some schedule social activities like exercise classes, crafting, or dance. Some organizations even provide adult day care for seniors.

Many local recreation centers offer classes for seniors and/or discounts on entrance fees or passes.

Depending on the needs of your parents, you may find many of their needs fulfilled by a community senior program.

## Long-Term Care Insurance

Many insurance agents and financial advisors represent companies who offer long-term care (LTC) insurance. Check with your agent or advisor. Some organizations such as credit unions, clubs, retirement groups, and labor unions offer long-term care insurance to their members as a benefit of membership.

There are also insurance agents who specialize in long-term care policies. I really like LTCPartner. com. Jack Lenenberg has been a specialist in this area for over 18 years and is an independent agent, meaning he can provide you with the policy that best fits your parents' needs (and yours too). If nothing else, check out his website for good information on the specifics of long-term care insurance.

One leading provider of LTC insurance is Genworth. Their website (Genworth.com) has many good thought-provoking resources on how to choose LTC insurance, what it costs, and how to know what kind of care to assume in your planning.

Remember, one of the biggest myths of the senior years is that Medicare covers long-term care. It does not. Seniors must use their own funds for this type of care and it can get very expensive.

## Medical Providers

Although many elders have a doctor who they have trusted for years, many of those doctors have retired or your parents have moved to a new area. I recommend that you seek out medical providers that specialize in geriatrics. Many hospitals or clinics have senior health centers where doctors, nurse practitioners, and other providers are focused on coordinated care for elders. This offers huge benefits over seeing a specialist for every type of care needed, especially if you are not there to coordinate it.

Many assisted living and nursing care residences have geriatric physician groups that make calls to the residence to see patients on a weekly, monthly, or periodic basis. If one of these groups is available for your parent in a senior residence, it's usually a very good option for routine care. Elders can be referred to a specialist, if needed, by the geriatric group. In such cases, you have a better chance of coordinated care than with individual medical providers. Ask at your parents' residence if this option is available.

## Housing

If your parent needs care at home after a hospital stay, needs to receive care in a rehabilitation center, or needs to move to assisted living or full nursing care, the hospital or clinic social worker can provide referrals to home care agencies, hospice agencies, and rehab centers. They often will give you a list to call or to visit. DO THIS! You will want to make sure that your loved ones are going to a place or being cared for by a group of people who are kind and who meet their needs. See questions to ask in the chapter on housing. The hospital or rehab center social workers are great resources for, not only housing options, but also home care agencies, hospice agencies, and many other senior services. Use these helpful folks for all you can!

Senior guides/publications are great for identifying retirement residences of all kinds.

They often provide a grid chart showing which kinds of services each residence provides. Senior centers, municipal services dedicated to aging/ seniors, and/or state departments on aging also can be resources for different housing options. Senior publications also list contractors who can retrofit homes for senior needs.

If your parents are going to live with you, check into adult day care services. Most community and senior centers can direct you to places that provide care for seniors during the day while the primary caregivers are working.

There are consultants who specialize in assistance with senior housing assessment and placement. You may find one of these through the local senior center or state department on aging.

The wide array of options in housing may seem daunting but, remember, your first priority is FIT – the intersection of what your parents want and need with what is available for their budget.

To get an idea about costs for senior housing options, Genworth Insurance has a great online tool. Go to Genworth.com and search for "Cost of Care." You can select your state or the state where your parents live and the tool provides average annual costs for a variety of care options (home health aides, adult day care, assisted living, and nursing home care).

## Medical Insurance

While Medicare pays for much of a senior's healthcare, most seniors obtain supplemental insurance to pay for the copays, coinsurance, and deductibles that Medicare does not cover. Some seniors opt out of traditional Medicare and enroll in a Medicare Advantage plan that covers the patient via an HMO or network. The very best starting point for this investigation is Medicare.gov. Look for the sections on supplemental health insurance and prescription drug plans. You can search by your local area or, more specifically, by personal information.

Remember – all Medicare supplemental plans are standardized across the country and are identified by a letter (like A, D, or N). Each plan offers different benefits but the benefits are standard across the country within that plan. For example, Plan A provides the same benefits if you live in Maine or Hawaii. Plan A differs from Plan N (etc.) in the type of coverage it provides.

Many seniors use the AARP/United Healthcare supplemental insurance plans. The AARP website, AARPHealthcare.com, has sections on insurance offerings of all kinds – health, supplemental, dental, vision, etc. You can search plans and their prices if you enter some basic qualifying information.

There are many providers of supplemental Medicare insurance. The best plan for your elder is the one that covers the most areas of their individual needs at the cost that they can afford. Start with the Medicare website and go from there.

Medicare does not cover vision, dental, or hearing costs. If your parent does not have this kind of insurance via their retirement program from work, you may want to check out supplemental plans that offer insurance or discounts in these areas too.

## Social Security

The Social Security website (SocialSecurity.gov) offers information on benefits and office locations, has online applications as well as a retirement estimator. You can also call Social Security at 1-800-772-1213.

## Hospice

Hospice care is for patients who have been diagnosed as terminally ill with a life expectancy of six months or less. Original Medicare covers Medicare-approved hospice costs, regardless of whether your loved one is insured under Original Medicare or has a Medicare Advantage plan. Go to Medicare.gov and search for hospice. There is a list of what's covered under the hospice benefit as well as a thorough description of how hospice works.

There are national organizations that offer hospice information and support. American Hospice Foundation (AmericanHospice.org) has a wealth of information for caregivers and hospice patients. The Hospice Foundation of America provides information to families on end of life and hospice care as well as dealing with grief. Visit Hospice-Foundation.org. The National Association of Home Care & Hospice has some very helpful resources on their website (www.nahc.org) under the Consumer Information tab. They have a hospice patient's bill of rights, hospice fact sheets, and a listing of hospice and home care state associations.

As I mentioned in the chapter on hospice, the book *Final Gifts* by Maggie Callanan and Patricia Kelley is a must-read for those families experiencing hospice for the first time. The authors are hospice nurses and offer extensive support and wisdom for the whole end-of-life experience.

**Veterans Benefits**

Many elders are veterans or spouses of veterans. The VA pays a variety of benefits for veterans or their widow(er)s. Go to Benefits.VA.gov and read their publications to check for benefits and eligibility for your parents. The veteran or their surviving spouse must need extensive assistance with ADLs and must be housebound to qualify for the aid and attendance benefit. Many benefits have a needs-based qualifier as well. Income thresholds, medical expenses, service during an active war, and other factors are used to compute whether or not a veteran or surviving spouse is qualified. There are often state veteran advocate agencies that help navigate benefits and services for veterans and their spouses. Good news for tech-savvy folks: the VA now allows you to apply for and manage your benefits online. This is a big step in simplifying life for veterans and their caretakers. You can also visit local VA offices near you for information. Applying for VA benefits is often complicated and very time-consuming so perseverance pays!

## Charities

There are many charitable organizations that accept used items and clothing from seniors. For furniture and household items, groups like ARC, Goodwill, and DAV (Disabled Veterans) will pick up the donated items at your loved ones' residence. This can be handy if you have a large amount or want to donate big and bulky items. Remember, many organizations that benefit the homeless and victims of domestic violence have thrift stores willing to take many of the items that seniors are parting with as they prepare to move to a smaller residence. Consider food banks for toiletries and food as well.

Clothing can be donated to the charities above, or if it is usable for business attire, you may want to consider Dress for Success. Visit their website at DressForSuccess.org to see what they are currently accepting at locations near you.

### Alzheimer's Disease

Many seniors are diagnosed with Alzheimer's disease and other debilitating dementias. This is such an extensive topic that it deserves its own set of resources. The Alzheimer's Association is a great place to start (go to Alz.org or call 1-800-272-3900) for educational information, resources, and advice on this disease as well as help for those caring for an Alzheimer's patient. There are numerous helpful books for caregivers and loved ones that walk you through the different stages of dementia, recognizing symptoms and finding ways to connect with your loved ones along this journey. I heartily recommend that you read as many of these as you can. Attend the free workshops offered by the Alzheimer's Association and find a caregivers' support group. This is one path where you will need to reach out for resources from beginning to end.

# Acknowledgments

I would like to thank my husband, Keith, for his loving support and encouragement despite the times when it was not convenient or easy. He is my best friend and my very best sounding board. I've seen Keith at the hardest of times – having to tell his dad over and over (since he forgot each time) that he was dying of cancer. My heart swells with love every time I think of the strength and love it took to show such support and compassion.

Our daughter, Emily, has been such a champ throughout the years, watching her grandparents endure and progress through the aging process. She once described her parents by saying, "My daddy does computers and my mommy does Grammy's insurance." Her sweet temperament, loving personality, and her clever observations have helped her to make the most of her time with her grandparents. Thanks, Emily, for your gifts of perspective.

My brother, Jim, is my partner in crime for Mom's care. He is always up for a new idea, a better way to do things, or a good laugh. I couldn't have done any of this without his partnership, his love, and his support. It pays to have a great partner sibling. I've had the best.

My sister-in-law, Harl, is the original impetus for writing this book. She encouraged me to share what I'd learned and insisted that there were others struggling with the same topics. When I needed a cheerleader, Harl ran on to the field.

My in-laws, Elaine and Jim Blankenship, have been so loving and accepting of my part in their care. Their embrace of my ideas, suggestions, and advocacy on their behalf is touching. It has been an honor to be a part of their older years.

Thank you to Marc Thibodeau, my amazing illustrator, for helping me tell the story in pictures. Judith Briles, my book shepherd, deserves many thanks for her insights, and for holding my hand. Much gratitude goes to both my editor, James Hallman, for keeping me on track – but with my own voice, and to my designer, Nick Zelinger, for his spot-on talent, patience, and wise counsel.

– SAB

# About the Author

Suzanne Asaff Blankenship's experience with eldercare came the hard way – by doing it. Suzanne is in the second decade of managing her mother's care and has been a co-caretaker for her in-laws for the past 4+ years. After countless conversations, discussions, commiserations, and requests for advice, Suzanne finally gave up and wrote a book.

Suzanne has spent her 20-year corporate career in marketing and customer service, leading and training teams at The Coca-Cola Company, Bueno Foods, and Ogilvy & Mather as well as at her own consulting firm, Parkin & Blankenship. She worked with diverse clients in hospitality, food & beverage, cinema, retail, convenience, tourism, technology, manufacturing, and gaming. Once immersed in eldercare, Suzanne found customer service and advocacy in that arena immensely lacking. Determined to improve the experience for her elderly parent and in-laws, Suzanne developed tools, identified resources, and put together organized plans for each different scenario as they developed.

From Texas originally, Suzanne now calls Colorado home. She believes in advocacy, the importance of family, and the need for balance in life. Humor is her favorite resource.

# How to Connect with Suzanne

Suzanne helps you navigate eldercare
in many forms:

- Workshops for organizations, businesses, churches, and groups

- Speaking engagements, topics include:
    - **Calling Their Bluff:** *How to identify your elder's needs and put together a plan to help*
    - **Getting Their House in Order:** *Finding, reviewing, and refreshing the critical documents in eldercare*
    - **I've Got Your Back:** *The importance of advocacy for your elders*

- Online at SuzanneBlankenship.com

- Blog posts from The Eldercare Navigator

- Eldercare topics covered on frequent podcasts

- Deep dives into individual topics available for online purchase

On Facebook: Suzanne Blankenship –
Author

On Pinterest: Suzanne Blankenship

**Suzanne can be contacted at:**

**SuzanneABlankenship@gmail.com**
**SuzanneBlankenship.com**
**TheEldercareNavigator.com**

CPSIA information can be obtained
at www.ICGtesting.com
Printed in the USA
BVHW091307170522
637236BV00012B/778